Drugstore
COLLECTIBLES

A WALLACE-HOMESTEAD PRICE GUIDE

Drugstore COLLECTIBLES

PATRICIA McDANIEL

Wallace-Homestead Book Company
Radnor, Pennsylvania

On the cover (see diagram): **(A)** *Batcheller Air Purifier, $33.00;* **(B)** *Hamburger Bruft Thee (Hamburg Breast Tea), $27.00;* **(C)** *Princess Pat Lipstick on advertising card, $12.00;* **(D)** *Gets-It Corn and Callous Remover advertising vase, $175.00;* **(E)** *Noxema Complexion Lotion, $8.50;* **(F)** *Rexall ceramic apothecary jar, $400.00;* **(G)** *Toneco Stomach Bitters, $65.00;* **(H)** *cobalt apothecary bottle with glass label, $250.00;* **(I)** *666 Medicines advertising fan (medicines listed on back), $45.00;* **(J)** *Sealtex Bandage, $10.00;* **(K)** *ceramic mortar and pestle, $15.00;* **(L)** *French Lick Salts, $45.00;* **(M)** *Snow Facial Depilatory, $40.00;* **(N)** *5-cc apothecary medicine measure, $10.00;* **(O)** *Dr. A. W. Chase's Catarrh Powder, $15.00;* **(P)** *Smith Brothers Cough Syrup (bottle and box), $18.00;* **(Q)** *One Night Corn Salve, $18.00;* **(R)** *Durante's Frogletts cough-drop tin, $150.00;* **(S)** *Murray & Nickell Cramp Bark, $8.00.*

Copyright © 1994 by Patricia McDaniel
All Rights Reserved
Published in Radnor, Pennsylvania 19089, by Wallace-Homestead,
a division of Chilton Book Company

Photography by Harry Rinker, Jr.
Designed by Anthony Jacobson

Manufactured in the United States of America

Library of Congress Cataloging-in-Publication Data

McDaniel, Patricia,
    Drugstore collectibles / Patricia McDaniel.
        p.   cm.
    Includes index.
    ISBN 0-87069-691-2
        1. Drugstores—Collectibles—United States—Catalogs.
    2. Antiques—United States—History—19th century—Catalogs.
    3. Antiques—United States—History—20th century—Catalogs.
    I. Title.
NK807.M38   1994
381'.456151'075—dc20
                                                                    94-1495
                                                                    CIP

1 2 3 4 5 6 7 8 9 0   3 2 1 0 9 8 7 6 5 4

To my mother,

Vera Hyde McDaniel

Remember the campaign buttons . . .

———————

Contents

Acknowledgments

According to Robert Frost's poem: "Two roads diverged into a wood and I took the one less traveled by, and that made all the difference . . ."

The path of writing a book is *definitely* not straight. First of all, my Aunt Bessie (Hyde) instilled in me a love of words and writing. A special thanks to Harry Rinker for continuing me on my journey. Helen Cook, Pat Morse, and Earl Smith all provided time, effort, and encouragement. Thanks to Susan Keller, my editor, for her help in developing this book. Kudos go to many individuals—a silent thanks for all of your support. Thanks also to a great many members of the Earlham College community of Richmond, Indiana, who contributed verbal encouragement.

Thanks to Jim Chagares of Chagares Photography in Richmond, Indiana. He was able to photographically capture an effervescent Lilly (my Labrador/Airedale).

To Ken and Katharine Jacobson of Richmond, Indiana—need I say more?

CHAPTER ONE

Collecting Vintage Drugstore Products

Vintage pharmaceuticals and related items are currently being sought by collectors. Although this is a relatively new field of collecting, with the parameters not fully established, the popularity of merchandise that appeared behind the pharmaceutical counter and on the shelves of the small, individually owned drugstore seems to be growing.

Vintage medicines and other pharmaceutical products constitute a part of American social history. They help recall a time when life was simple and the pungent odor of herbs and oils permeated the pharmacy. Nowadays, it's hard to find a drugstore where the pharmacist is not only counting pills for a prescription, but also measuring and sacking a scoop of nails or mixing a soda while the waitress is on lunch break.

Each item collected can provide a glimpse of pre-1960 America. The label and instructions from a bottle or box of vintage medicine can reveal much about how life was lived and illness attended to in the days before nuclear medicine and other medical advances.

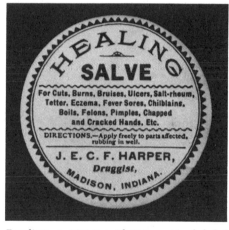

Reading a vintage pharmaceutical label can prove enlightening.

A sense of humor as well as a sense of the times is often evident in the claims made, names used, and illustrations found on many bygone medicines. Fanciful names such as Konjola, Dr. Drake's Glesso, and Tan-A-Wa will conjure memories for some and evoke curiosity in others. Many collectors will be surprised to learn that products such as Lydia Pinkham's Vegetable Compound and Dr. Kilmer's Swamp Root are still

1

Sometimes the graphics on a vintage pharmaceutical label are as interesting as the information included.

available today. The world of vintage pharmaceuticals is truly eye-opening and, in large part, remains to be explored.

While there is a definite demand for old drugstore items, in my opinion very little has been disseminated in regard to pricing, collecting hints, or how to start a pharmacy collection. Recently, I selected an assortment of pharmaceutical items and decided to test this hypothesis.

After driving a distance of approximately seventy-five miles from my shop in Indiana, I began to visit antique shops and malls. It was my intention to offer the items as a collection to the proprietors. (This is a sophisticated antique-collecting community with a wide range of dealers and merchandise.) Questions asked at each shop included the following: (1) Are you interested in purchasing a collection of vintage phar-

maceuticals? (2) If so, what are you willing to pay for the lot? and (3) If you are not interested, why not?

Responses from the twenty dealers varied. Some of them felt they could not resell the items because most of the boxes and bottles lacked unusual colors and graphics. Other, more informed dealers noted specific faults that would detract from the value of some of the items. The apothecary bottle, for example, had a crack in its stopper and lacked a pontil mark (the indentation left after a hand-blown bottle is sheared from the mold). Hand-blown bottles are usually older and more valuable than bottles without a pontil mark. An aspirin bottle contained an encircled "R" trademark symbol on its lid, meaning it most likely dated from the 1950s or later and so wasn't as valuable as an older medicine bottle might have been.

Most of the dealers simply stated that they didn't know what to pay for the lot. They were unable to price any of the items individually, with the possible exception of the 1906 cardboard box containing crushed mandrake root (valuable because of its displayed date) and the tin of Dr. Lyons tooth powder (tins are popular among many types of collectors), so they didn't know what to pay for the lot in order to make a profit.

Clearly there is a need for information on vintage pharmaceuticals; this book has been written to provide such information. Not only does the book list prices and descriptions for over 30 categories of pharmaceutical-related collectibles, including everything from asthma remedies and dietary supplements to laxatives and women's toiletries, but it also tries to shed some light on the activity of collecting itself. Who currently collects vintage drugstore items? Where can such items be found? What makes an item worth collecting? These questions and other collecting concerns will be explored here in Chapter 1. The alphabetical listing of categories is contained in Chapter 2, while Chapter 3 provides more descriptions and prices of collectibles, this time organized by chemical and pharmaceutical companies, and Chapter 4 organizes several drugstore items into four sample collections. In addition, "collecting hints" containing specific information about an item or an aspect of collecting are scattered throughout the book, and a list of medical museums and resources for collectors are included in the back of the book.

Who Collects Vintage Drugstore Items

As an antique shop owner who is a purveyor of old pharmaceutical items, I have been able to observe people as they browse, compare prices, and purchase items. I have seen pharmacists, doctors, nurses, dentists, and individuals in allied health occupations make frequent visits to see if new items have been placed on my shelves. And by no means are these the only customers interested in vintage drugstore items; these collectibles are starting to attract a broad variety of potential collectors. For example, Hadacol was a dietary supplement manufactured by the LeBlanc Corporation in Lafayette, Louisiana. The following individuals might have an interest in a 1940s bottle of Hadacol: (1) individuals within the medical profession; (2) prop masters and set decorators for movies, plays, and television; (3) curators of museums; (4) libraries; (5) someone searching for items that maintain a color scheme of blue and white; (6) residents of Louisiana who advertise on a national basis seeking items indicative of their native state; (7) individuals with the name "LeBlanc"; and (8) individuals who purchase "Hadacol" on a whim because it reminds them of the saying "Hadda call it something."

Collectors with medical or pharmaceutical knowledge often pursue collecting with intensity. A couple from California have visited my shop at approximately the same time of year for two consecutive years. Both are pharmacists with a large pharmaceutical chain. They are moderate-to-advanced collectors who spend their vacations in the Midwest hoping to find additional items for their drugstore collection. Their mélange is rapidly encroaching upon every corner of their home, but they are still trying to locate that one elusive item for their large revolving display case. I learned a great deal during the three days they spent at my shop on their last visit. They shared such tidbits as when certain companies merged with other, existing companies and when products changed their logo, label, design, color, size, or bottle. Each of their detailed notebooks contain references about their existing collection so that they can avoid duplication when purchasing additional vintage pharmaceuticals.

One of my more unusual tasks as a shop owner has been providing props for period movies. Both prop masters and set decorators prefer to purchase vintage items because the box, bottle, and printing contain a patina not available when items are replicated. It is often necessary for these people to purchase items in quantity. A prop master may need many items for one movie because of the breakage factor when items are handled, dropped, or thrown. Set decorators need "controlled" multi-

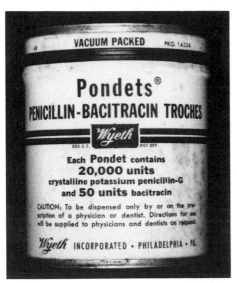

VACUUM PACKED PKG. 1A324

48

Pondets®
PENICILLIN-BACITRACIN TROCHES

Wyeth

REG. U.S.   PAT. OFF.

Each **Pondet** contains
20,000 units
crystalline potassium penicillin-G
and **50 units** bacitracin

CAUTION: To be dispensed only by or on the prescription of a physician or dentist. Directions for use
will be supplied to physicians and dentists on request.

Wyeth INCORPORATED • PHILADELPHIA • PA.

Pondets Penicillin-Bacitracin Troches are an example of vintage prescription medicines that might be used to stock the shelves of an old-time pharmacy on a television or movie set.

ples of items because the old drugstore was never stocked in perfect order. There might have been seven boxes of Foley Pills, five bottles of Garglette, three jars of white petroleum jelly, six cans of Pondets Penicillin-Bacitracin Troches, and three tubes of Hart's Nasal Jelly.

Other people have their own personal agendas for why they collect old drugstore items. It's a continual challenge to keep up with this growing field, yet the sense of wonderment evoked when individuals share their personal stories is more than worth the effort.

Starting a Collection

Many small pharmacies have transferred their prescriptions to the huge sprawling megastores of the 1990s. Individuals are beginning to wax nostalgic when they happen upon a now-defunct product at an auction, garage sale, or in their great uncle's medicine chest. Products manufactured before the Pure Food and Drug Act of 1906 are especially coveted by collectors. Patent medicines, items from a specific pharmaceutical company, dental products, medicinal tins, and shaving paraphernalia evoke nostalgia.

While some collections are made up of just a few items, most often a collection includes ten or more products grouped together. Here are several suggestions to consider when starting a drugstore collection.

1. Buy the best you can afford. (It is wise to invest a few more dollars for an item in pristine condition if at all possible.)

2. Look for excellent graphics on the packaging of items. Only you, the collector, can determine if it is better to invest in a pre-1890 intricately designed Somers Brothers medicinal tin with the woman's features crazed or to purchase an Art-Deco style tin in mint condition (assuming that you want eventually to have items from both decades in your collection and money is no object).

3. The condition of the pharmaceutical item is of utmost importance when making a purchase. An item in mint condition enhances a collection and will increase in value at a higher rate than a similar item which is incomplete or damaged. Consider the following example using a bottle of Hill's Nose Drops:

- A full bottle with a complete label, dropper, instruction sheet, and box is valued at $5.00.

- A box and full bottle with a complete label and box but without instructions and dropper is valued at $3.50.

- A full bottle with a complete label is valued at $3.00.

- An empty box in mint condition would be valued at $2.00.

- An empty box with a price sticker or price written by the dealer would have a value of $1.00.

- An empty bottle with no label would be worth 50¢. If the bottle was not embossed, there would be no value to the bottle.

This same procedure, with slight modifications depending upon the specific item being evaluated, could be employed whenever a purchase is made.

4. Do not purchase anything that is rusty or damp.

5. Whenever you purchase an item, request that the seller remove the price tag or erase any new price written in pencil. Make this request only if you are serious about buying the item and be clear that you only want the item if the price removal is successful. There have been many times when I have refrained

A Hill's Nose Drops package that includes a bottle, stopper, and box is valued at $3.

The value of one of these empty mint-condition boxes, when sold alone, is $2.

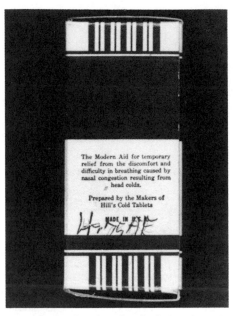

Because this box has the dealer's price written on it, its value has diminished to $1.

This bottle is embossed, so even though the label is damaged, the bottle can still be valued at 50¢.

from a purchase because the dealer has refused to comply with this request.

6. Buy a variety of pharmaceutical products and consider placing several similar items together on a shelf for increased visual effect. (If your budget is strained, buy bottles in their original boxes and then remove the bottle and place it in front of the box.)

7. Purchase pharmaceutical products from a variety of time periods.

8. Comparison shop, and don't buy on impulse unless the item is rare.

9. Keep a written inventory of your purchases.

10. Take Polaroid photos or a video of your collection if documentation is needed for insurance purposes.

11. If prices are reasonable (or just a bit steep), purchase several extras. Dupli-

cates will make excellent trading material. Remember there will always be collectors more advanced than you, but in the next five to ten years your "extras" may be just what another collector is seeking. Your "stash" or "cache" will come in handy.

12. Avoid purchasing products from individuals who advertise "warehouse finds." These are likely to be advertised at flea markets, some shops, and especially in regional and national antique publications. "Dr. Blume" from Chicago has made so many "house calls" that he is no longer welcome.

13. Determine how much space will be allocated for your collection and buy accordingly.

14. Consider collecting vintage products from foreign countries. Many early British and Canadian tins command high prices.

Taking a Konjola bottle out of its original box and displaying the two items together is one way collectors can get the most for their money.

15. Be wary of including new items (especially reproduction tins) in a collection. Common sources for these products are Japan, Taiwan, and China. Reproductions will never have value to a collector who is a purist with regard to vintage pharmaceutical material.

Dating Items in Your Collection

It is usually quite difficult to ascertain the exact age of a drugstore collectible, but there are many places to look for hints as to when your collectible was produced. If the medicine is in its original cardboard box, read the box, the medicine's label, and any instruction sheet found inside the box. There the copyright date, patent number, or even the style of graphics and lettering can give you clues as to the date of the item. Hair and clothing styles of people depicted on the packaging can also provide valuable information. Zip codes have only been in existence since 1963,

so an address that includes a zip code is a telltale sign that the item was made in the 1960s or later.

In some cases, research is the only method for approximating dates. Investigating when certain medicines were used and the history of certain companies and products may prove helpful. Don't overlook the value of talking to a pharmacist who has been in business for a number of years or consulting regional manufacturing directories available at some local libraries and company headquarters.

Where to Find Vintage Drugstore Items

With a little bit of effort, vintage pharmaceuticals can be found in some unusual places. You'll need to muster your spirit of adventure, though, because traveling off the beaten path is often required. Just remember that even though flea markets, auctions and thrift stores may be the most obvious places to look for old drugstore items, they are not always the best. Here are some suggestions for innovative ways to locate drugstore collectibles:

1. If medicinal bottle collecting is your passion, and you're not as concerned with labels, get permission to dig in (and around) an old outhouse, an abandoned farmhouse, or a landfill.

2. The classified advertising section of most newspapers contains a "Misc. For Sale" category. Check for people selling personal belongings and/or having yard sales. Once you get to the sale (or to the seller's house), don't hesitate to inquire about items that are not priced or not placed on tables. (How many people would think of selling Aunt Nellie's tooth powder, corn salve, or tins of rouge?)

3. If you know of someone who's moving (especially an elderly person), volunteer to help clean out the person's home. You never know what you might find in the medicine chest, basement, attic, shed, or closet.

These are just a few suggestions. With a bit of enthusiasm and ingenuity, you're sure to discover your own methods and haunts for drugstore treasure hunting.

Helping someone elderly move or inquiring about personal items when at a garage sale may result in finds such as this salve tin with excellent graphics.

Current Collecting Trends

Little research has been conducted to determine what items are being coveted by collectors. It has been difficult (if not virtually impossible) to produce a specific state-of-the-market report. The scant information provided here has been based upon sales in my antique shop and my experience described earlier of trying to peddle an assortment of old drugstore items to area dealers.

Anything prophylactic is popular.

Condom tins, cardboard boxes, and dispensers sell quickly. Products which are now classified as pertaining to "safe sex" are desirable. There is often a tongue-in-cheek attitude to collecting these products.

Collectors are always on the lookout for old feminine hygiene products, including sanitary napkin dispensers and their ornamentation. These machines are now strategically placed in household bathrooms, be they contemporary or old-fashioned in decor. Some dealers and collectors have literally removed the metal "nurse holding boxes of Kotex" from metal display racks still in use from the 1930s and 1940s.

Apothecary bottles with gold labels under glass are avidly sought. The labels are quite fragile, and it is difficult to locate one that has no crazing, chipping, or peeling of the glass label. Bottles with pontil marks (an indentation indicating the bottle is hand-blown) command higher prices. It is not uncommon for collectors to visit my shop hoping to find apothecary bottles that will complete their graduated set.

Any medical tins in mint condition with pre-1930s graphics barely have to be dusted, priced, and displayed in a shop before they are sold. There are many eager people who collect nothing but tins.

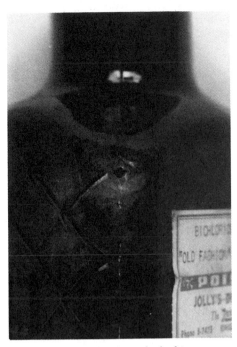

This photo demonstrates why looking at several photos of an item before buying by mail-order is wise. Closer inspection of the poison bottle reveals a small defect that diminishes the item's value. Even with the defect, the bottle is valued at $125. If it had been in mint condition, it might have sold for $250 to $300.

Large cobalt embossed poison bottles like this one continue to be popular and fetch good prices.

So-called patent medicines are sought after—especially those that have a cork stopper, embossed lettering on the bottle, the contents or pictures on the front or back labels, or the original box. (**Collecting hint:** It is important never to remove the original price from a box. This also applies to any other vintage collectible with the original price on it.)

Items marked "poison" are quite valuable. Ribbed, cobalt, and triangular bottles are scarce and thus desirable. Large bottles command high prices. (**Collecting hint:** When purchasing a bottle, examine it carefully—preferably in bright light. If you are purchasing a bottle by mail, request several photos of the item (from several angles), rather than just one photo.

It will be interesting to hear what other readers, collectors, and dealers have to share regarding current collecting trends. Thoughts and comments are appreciated.

Projected Collecting Trends

There is no way for one individual to accurately predict what items will be "hot" in the next three to five years. As an author, dealer, collector, and observer, I feel that the following categories will gain momentum.

A Baker's Dozen of Pharmaceutical Predictions

1. The *Physician's Desk Reference (PDR)*, currently in its 47th edition, is issued annually. It will garner popularity because of collectors' continual fascination with old books and their insatiable thirst for information pertaining to old-time ailments and their cures.

2. Selected physicians, dentists, and opticians already decorate their offices and home with vintage medical equipment, scales, and medicines. This trend will continue as baby boomers become more nostalgic.

3. Spouses of health-care givers will continue to purchase medical-related items for gifts throughout the year. Individuals, friends, and relatives will also follow this trend since it's easy to make purchases when a specific interest is known.

4. The mortar and pestle will remain popular because it is both decorative and utilitarian. These may be purchased in ceramic, wood, metal, glass, or plastic.

5. Tins with excellent graphics will continue to be in favor. Talc, cough drops, and laxative tins are quite expensive, but it is feasible to locate other choice tins including those which held razor blades, aspirin, and antacids. (**Collecting hint:** Any tin from before 1920 will be expensive.)

6. Tins that are unusual within the medical profession will become popular. They're, quite frankly, cheap and make excellent conversation pieces.

7. Executives who work for major pharmaceutical companies such as Eli Lilly

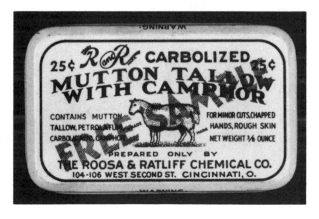

The Roosa and Ratliff Company of Cincinnati, Ohio, produced this sample tin, which is considered unusual because of the ewe depicted on the front, because it is a sample tin, and because of the inscription on the side, which reads "Good for sunburn, excellent for rectal irritation." You could say that this product is good for ailments from end to end.

will actively hone their collecting skills. Kibitzing about collecting and gloating smiles over coffee and lunch breaks will be very common at such companies.

8. Advertising giveaways from local pharmacies, chemical companies, and distributors of patent medicines will gain popularity.

9. Products with a specific personal name on them will begin to gain a foothold. A friend collects anything with "Dr. Jayne" simply because her name is "Jayne" and the medication named for the good doctor (e.g., Dr. Jayne's Cream Vermifuge) is spelled the same way.

10. Dovetail-jointed wooden boxes with a company's name embossed on the sides will rise in popularity. These are still relatively inexpensive, and what better repository for magazines, books, and toys? (**Collecting hint:** Do not varnish the box if you are considering it an investment. Purists will find this addition a definite distraction.)

11. Anything pertaining to prophylactics will continue to escalate in value. It's a "safe" wager that before long "The Golden Trojan" and "Roger (OK)" will be familiar to many collectors.

12. Any item that appears in a national decorating magazine will soon filter into shops and collections. (An item will be most desirable if its color and size parallel the item featured in the magazine.)

13. Buying and selling by mail order will increase as shopping time decreases. What better way to conserve time and increase one's pharmaceutical collection on a national scale?

Again, these predictions are merely speculative. It's a given that people will continue to collect and new categories will appear as items from previous collecting areas become difficult to locate or become too expensive.

How to Use This Book

The items described and pictured in this book are limited to American products that date roughly from the 1900s to the 1960s, with special emphasis given to items from the '20s, '30s, and '40s. Medicines and personal grooming items have been featured in an attempt to provide information that has not been widely available to collectors. Less detail is offered on topics such as advertising items, apothecary containers, and drugstore tins, because these subjects have been covered in other collecting books. Although medicinal products were distributed door-to-door in the United States by such companies as Rawleigh, McNess, Watkins, and Jewel Tea, this book covers only merchandise sold strictly in drugstores. Prices in the book are based on my experience as a shop owner and dealer and are meant only as a guideline.

Within each category in Chapters 2, 3, and 4, several items are listed, described, and priced. Here is a sample description:

Forni's Magolo, Dr. Peter Fahrney & Sons Co, Chicago, IL, Winnipeg, Manitoba, for relief of heartburn, acid indigestion, and sour stomach, "not laxative," 3½ fl oz, 5¾" × 1¾" × 1½" clear glass bottle, cream label with red letters, in cream and red 5¾"

× 1⅞″ × 1⅞″ cardboard box with red letters, name of company embossed on bottle side, full bottle **$8.00**

Here is a key to the information provided in the description:

Product Name: Forni's Magolo

Manufacturing Company: Dr. Peter Fahrney & Sons Co

Location of Company: Chicago, IL, Winnipeg, Manitoba

Purpose or Generic Name of Product: for relief of heartburn, acid indigestion, and sour stomach

Anything Quoted from Label: "not laxative"

Volume of Container: 3½ fl oz

Information about Container (colors, materials, dimensions, type of container): 5¾″ × 1¾″ × 1½″ clear glass bottle, cream label with red letters, in cream and red 5¾″ × 1⅞″ × 1⅞″ cardboard box with red letters

Any Special Information: name of company embossed on bottle side

Amount of Item in Container: full bottle

Price: $8.00

In addition to descriptions of individual products, each main category in Chapter 2: An Alphabetical Listing of Drugstore Collectibles, also contains some anecdotes or information about that type of collectible and applicable collecting hints. Many of the categories included, such as Cough and Cold Remedies, contain subcategories, such as Cold Tablets and Cough Syrups. If you're having trouble locating a specific type of product, consult the Index. A listing of chemical and pharmaceutical companies in Chapter 3 includes at least one product from each company. The list is a good starting place for collectors who want to focus on individual companies. The items in Chapter 4 are organized into four sample collections. The Collectors' Resources section, at the back of the book, includes clubs, museums, and periodicals valuable to the collector of drugstore items.

List of Abbreviations

caps	Capsules	fl	Fluid
Co	Company	N.F.	National Formulary
distr	Distributor or distributed	oz	Ounces
		reg.	Registered
Div	Division	tabs	Tablets
Inc	Incorporated	U.S.P.	United States Pharmacopeia
mfr	Manufactured or manufacturer	U.S. Pat. Off.	United States Patent Office
mfg	Manufacturing		

CHAPTER TWO

An Alphabetical Listing of Drugstore Collectibles

Advertising Items

Advertising articles were often given to pharmacy proprietors and customers to promote new products. These items could be as graphically interesting as an advertising mirror of the 1890s or an advertising calendar of the 1940s, or as simple as a pencil with the pharmacy's logo on it from the 1960s. Thermometers, ashtrays, rulers, and nail files were some of the gifts distributed to customers. Matchbooks with the pharmacy's name, address, and phone number were also often given either with a pack of cigarettes or simply as a courtesy. (A collection of matchcovers with the matches removed makes an interesting and inexpensive collectible when mounted as a group.)

Advertising counter displays constitute a more expensive area of collecting. Not only were the displays usually larger and more elaborate than the items they promoted, but there were also fewer counter displays than other advertising items, making the displays more rare and thus more desirable to collectors.

Electric Prescription Sign, mfr by Ohio Advertising Display Co, Cincinnati, OH, 96½″ × 13″ × 4″ white metal and plastic sign with blue letters **50.00**

"A History of Pharmacy in Pictures," presented by Parke, Davis & Co, George A. Bendor, editor, Robert A. Thom, artist. "Avicenna The 'Persian Galen' (80–1037 AD)," 16½″ × 20″ × 1½″ cardboard color picture with attached gray-and-white striped cardboard frame, black letters; "The Governor who Healed The Sick (1640 AD)," 16½″ × 20″ × 1½″ cardboard color picture with attached gray-and-white striped cardboard frame, black letters, price for each **45.00**

McKesson's First-Aid and Good Health Almanac with 1946 calendar, picture of movie stars advertising various products, compliments of Rea and Sullivan, Druggist, Royal Center, IN **15.00**

Penslar Remedies Advertising Sign, Penslar Almond and Cucumber Cream, "for chap-

Hadacol, advertising drinking glass, 3½″ × 2″ clear glass with red lettering and animal figures advertising Hadacol: "It's something to crow about," says a rooster. "Hadacol gives me a lot of spring," says a kangaroo, etc. **95.00**

ped, rough skin," picture of a woman sitting in living room holding bouquet of pink roses, 24″ × 50″ cardboard on a wooden 24″ × 50″ frame, two other interchangeable advertising signs behind one display **145.00**

Pepto-Bismol Standup, 16″ × 24″ brown, yellow, and red advertising sign with red and black letters, picture of a turkey's head; "If the big bird bites back—Pepto Bismol!" **30.00**

Pluto Concentrated Spring Water, "laxative—mix with regular water, Bottled at the Springs only, French Lick Springs Hotel Co, French Lick, IN, USA," picture of Pluto, red and devil-like with horns, tail, and sword, "awarded Gold Medal, Paris, 1900, St. Louis, 1904" **55.00**

Princess Pat, "The Powder with the Almond Base," oil on canvas 22″ × 26″ × 1″ advertising picture in wooden frame, princess wearing yellow and green dress, blue and

navy cloak, tiara on head, holding box of Princess Pat Powder and a powder puff **150.00**

Rexall Gypsy Cream, Rexall Drug Co, "sunburn cream," 20″ × 30″ cardboard advertising sign, picture of a woman with bad sunburn wearing bathing suit and holding a bottle of Gypsy Cream **18.00**

Rexall Products Clock, 42″ × 14″ × 4½″ blue and white plastic electric clock on wood frame, blue and white letters **55.00**

Round tin and glass Fahrenheit Thermometer advertising August Flower, "liver, indigestion, constipation," and German Syrup (Roshee's) for "coughs, colds, etc." **275.00**

Apothecary Equipment

Collecting apothecary equipment can be as limited or as expansive as the collector desires. Apothecary bottles are one of the most sought-after items of apothecary equipment, with graduated sets being especially desirable. Other factors that make an apothecary bottle valuable include a pontil mark (an indentation that signifies the bottle was hand-blown), a gold label (it is difficult to find one that is not crazed or chipped), and a company or product name embossed or inscribed on the bottle. Mortar and pestles are also popular. Care should be given when cleaning any apothecary equipment; there may be chemical residue which should be removed carefully.

Collecting hint: Sometimes a perfect glass stopper can be removed from a cracked apothecary bottle and used on a bottle in excellent condition. Thus, it is a good idea to purchase boxes of glass stoppers if they happen to become available. To loosen a glass stopper from a bottle, hold it under warm running water. If it remains stuck, leave it alone. Trying to force the stopper could result in one less bottle in your collection!

Mortar and pestle, 16-oz, 4″ clear glass mortar with 7″ clear glass pestle, set **22.00**

Scale, Rexall Drugs, 13″ × 13″ × 6 ″ metal balance scale with plates suspended from chains **165.00**

Stainless-Steel Scoop, Williamson, "for scooping/measuring of medicines," "Williamson" embossed in handle, one piece, 9¼″ from tip of handle to end of scoop, 5″ × 2½″ × 1½″ scoop **7.00**

Tin Scoop, ⅓-cup, 2¾″ × 2″ × 2″ curved tin handle soldered to flat back, rounded scoop **7.00**

Tin Scoop, ⅔-cup, 3¾″ × 3¼″ × 2″ two-piece tin scoop soldered together, small rounded tin handle soldered on flat back **12.00**

Tin Scoop, ⅔-cup, 3¼″ × 2¾″ × 2¾″ medicine scoop and measure, rounded tin scoop, rounded back attached to scoop "basin," "teacup"-type handle attached to back **9.00**

Asthma Remedies

Appliances as well as medicines were used to alleviate symptoms in asthma sufferers. The DeVilbiss Glass Nebulizer For Aerosol Therapy, for example, utilized water-, oil-, or glycerine-based solutions. Early companies that produced medical accessories provided explicit instructions for the care and use of their products. The third paragraph of "instructions for use" on the back of the Devilbliss box is typical of the detailed directions: "Keeping mouth wide open, place throat tube (A) just inside teeth and direct it toward the back of throat. Inhale deeply while compressing bulb."

Asthma medicines often had multiple uses. Felsol powders and tablets, for instance, were used to provide relief from bronchopulmonary distress, including symptomatic relief from asthma, anthracosis (miners' asthma), and whooping cough. Felsol was also considered an analgesic and antipyretic (fever reducer) that provided relief for pain and fever due to head colds, neuralgia, muscular aches, premenstrual tension, and rheumatic fever.

Breatheasy, Pascal Co Inc, Seattle, WA, "inhalant for asthma, to be used with Breatheasy Pyrex Nebulizer," 1-fl oz, 1¼″ × 3⅜″ × 1¼″ tan and red box with black, tan, and red letters, full unopened cellophane-wrapped box **7.50**

DeVilbiss #40 Nebulizer, The DeVilbiss Co, Somerset, PA, glass nebulizer with rubber bulb and stoppers for water-, oil-, or glyccrinc-based solutions, "for aerosol therapy," 7⅞″ × 2⅛″ × 3½″ red and white box **15.00**
unboxed **7.75**

DeVilbiss #145 Vaporizer, The DeVilbiss Co, Somerset, PA, 7″ × 5½″ round clear glass vaporizer jar, green and yellow label with black and yellow letters **20.00**

Felsol, American Felsol Co, Lorain, OH, "antiasthmatic analgesic tablets," 30 tabs, 2¾″

*Minton's Asthma Preparation, Minton's, Sidney, OH, 16-fl oz, 2½″ × 2½″ × 7″ clear glass bottle, tan label with black letters, "since 1895," ¾-full bottle **11.00***

Page's Inhalers, Consolidated Chemical Co, Grand Rapids, MI, "temporary relief of asthma," 20 medicated cigarettes in 1¼" × 2¼" × 3¼" white box with blue letters, full unopened box **8.00**

× 1½" × 1½" white box with brown letters, full bottle **5.50**

Histeen, The Kenton Pharm. Co Inc, Covington, KY, "relief of asthma, hay fever, etc.," 40 tabs, plastic cylinder in 1" × 3" × 1" tan and green box, instruction sheet, full cylinder **5.00**

IS-NO-MAR, Hoover Medicine Co, Des Moines, IA, "asthma remedy," 14-fl oz, 3" × 8½" × 1½" clear glass bottle, black and white label with black letters, "new label adopted June 1st, 1934," ½-full bottle **8.75**

Cough and Cold Remedies

Medicines for aches, pains, sniffles, fever, neuralgia, sneezes, runny noses, coughs, colds, and allergies all helped to fill one section of the drugstore. Some of these medicines contained narcotics, alcohol, or even chloroform. If the medicine did not eliminate the cough or cold, at least the patient could get adequate rest. **See also** Infant and Children Cough and Cold Products; Nasal Products; Rubs, Liniments, and Ointments; and Throat Products.

COLD, ALLERGY, AND HAY FEVER REMEDIES

Grove's Bromo Quinine line of remedies was the forerunner of contemporary decongestants specially formulated to alleviate the discomforts of allergies and hay fever. The word "cold" still appeared on many of these packages.

"New" 4-Way Cold Tablets (also manufactured by Grove), Rehisco, Anahist, and Impact were a few of the products that made the transition and specifically addressed symptoms associated with allergies.

Many cold and allergy medications contained ingredients that could cause drowsiness. The warning "If signs of drowsiness occur, do not drive or operate machinery" appeared on package after package.

Anahist, Anahist Co Inc, Yonkers, NY, "for symptomatic relief of colds/hay fever," 15 tabs, ¾" × 1" × ½" clear glass brown bottle with black metal lid in 2" × 1¼" × ¾" blue and white cardboard box with blue and white letters, instruction sheet, full bottle **5.00**

Antomine—Anti-histamine, Grove Laboratories Inc, St. Louis, MO, "for colds/hay fever," 12 tabs, 1½" × 2" × ½" red and white cardboard box with blue and white letters, only 8 tabs in box **3.00**

Bromo Quinine Cold Tablets, Grove Laboratories Inc, St. Louis, MO, "cold and sinus relief," package of 16 tabs in 1⅜" × 2" × ½" red and white cardboard box with black and white letters, 12 unopened cellophane-wrapped boxes **5.00 each**

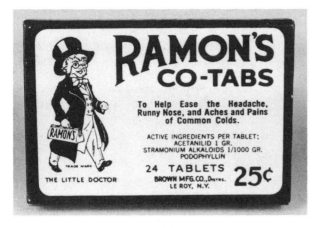

Ramon's Co-Tabs (Ramon's "The Little Doctor"), Brown Mfg Co Distr, LeRoy, NY, "to help ease the headache, runny nose and aches and pains of common colds," 24 tabs, 1⅞" × 2⅝" × ⅜" box, full unopened **5.75**

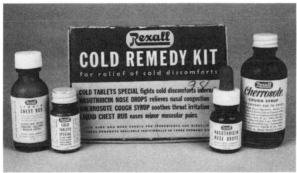

Rexall Cold Remedy Kit, Rexall Drug Co, Los Angeles, Boston, St. Louis, USA, "for relief of cold discomforts," 4" × 5¼" × 1½" blue and gray cardboard box containing the following: Cherrosote Cough Syrup, "for coughs due to colds," 2-fl oz, 3¾" × 1¼" clear brown glass bottle with white metal lid; Liquid Chest Rub, "relieves local surface congestion, eases minor muscle soreness,"

1-fl oz, 3" × 1" clear brown glass bottle with white plastic lid; Cold Tablets Special, "for relief of simple headache and minor muscular pain accompanying colds," 10 tabs, 2" × ¾" clear brown glass bottle with white metal lid; Nasothricin Nose Drops, "nasal decongestant antibiotic," ⅓-oz, 2" × ⅞" dark brown glass bottle with dropper lid; whole kit **25.00**

Campho-Lyptus Cold Capsules, Green Co Distr, Chicago, IL, "relieves minor muscular aches, pains, simple headaches and neuralgia due to colds," 25 tabs, 1⅞" × 2¾" × ⅜" red, green, and white metal box with black and white letters **3.75**

Candettes Cold Tablets, Family Products Dept, Chas. Pfizer & Co Inc, New York, NY, "for fast relief of sinus congestion, headaches, and similar cold discomforts," 24 tabs. 2¼" × 1¼" × ¾" clear brown bottle with blue metal lid in 2½" × 1½" × 1" blue and orange cardboard box with

orange and white letters, instruction sheet, full unopened bottle **4.75**

Coricidin, Schering Corp, Bloomfield, NJ, "for symptomatic relief of colds and accompanying aches, pains, fever, and for simple headaches," 25 tabs, 2½" × 1" clear glass bottle with clear plastic flip-top lid, red and white label with red and white letters, ½-full bottle **5.00**

CoVac (Ramon's—The Little Doctor) Cold and Hayfever Tablets, Brown Mfg Co, Distr, Leroy, NY, "anti-histaminic analgesic relief of colds/hay fever," 24 tabs, 1¾" ×

$2\frac{3}{4}'' \times \frac{1}{4}''$ red and white metal box with gray, white, and red letters, picture of "Little Doctor" on back, full unopened box **7.00**

Direxin Decongestant Tablets, Whitehall Laboratories Inc, New York, NY, 18 tabs, $2\frac{1}{4} \times \frac{3}{8}''$ plastic vial with clear plastic pop-top, brown and white label with yellow and brown letters, full unopened **6.00**

Fisher's Laxative Quinine Cold Tablets, Fisher Products Co Inc, Richmond, IN, "acts as a tonic as well as a cold remedy," 12 tabs, $1\frac{1}{4}'' \times 1\frac{3}{4}'' \times \frac{1}{4}''$ yellow metal box with black letters, full unopened **7.80**

4-Way Cold Tablets, Grove Laboratories, St. Louis, MO, Div of Bristol-Myers Co, "fast acting relief of cold distress/sinus congestion," 50 tabs, $3' \times 1\frac{1}{2}'' \times 1''$ clear glass bottle with white metal lid, white label with orange, blue, and white letters, full unopened **3.50**

Haywood Tablets, Pfeiffer Chemical Co, New York, St. Louis, "for the relief of the discomfort of some of the symptoms accompanying common colds," 25 tabs, $1\frac{1}{4}'' \times 2\frac{1}{4}'' \times \frac{1}{2}''$ white cardboard box with light and dark blue letters, instruction sheet, full box **3.80**

Histo-plus Antishistamine Analgesic Compound, Anahist Co Inc, Yonkers, NY, "for symptomatic relief of colds, simple headaches, minor aches and pains," 15 tabs, $2\frac{3}{4}'' \times \frac{3}{4}''$ clear glass cylinder with plastic pop-off lid in $3'' \times \frac{7}{8}'' \times \frac{7}{8}''$ gray and white cardboard box with blue and white letters, instruction sheet, full cylinder **3.80**

Impact Continuous Action Decongestant, Approved Pharmaceutical Corp, Syracuse Distr, NY, "provides relief from congestion due to head colds, hay fever, sinus," 15 timed caps, $2\frac{1}{4}'' \times 1''$ clear glass bottle with plastic flip-top lid, white label with blue and black letters, full unopened bottle **6.50**

Kriptin Anti-histamine Tablets, Whitehall Pharmacal Co, New York, NY, USA, "new relief for colds and hay fever," 12 tabs, $1\frac{1}{4}'' \times 1\frac{3}{4}'' \times \frac{1}{4}''$ blue and white metal box with blue letters, full unopened box **5.50**
Display: $2\frac{3}{4}'' \times 3\frac{3}{4}'' \times 1\frac{1}{8}''$ blue and white cardboard box, display box only **5.00**

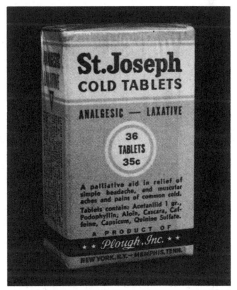

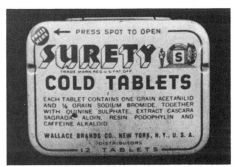

Surety Cold Tablets, Wallace Brands Co, New York, NY, USA, distr, "recommended for the relief of minor colds, simple headaches and minor muscular aches and pains due to common colds, tablets are mildly laxative," 12 tabs, $1\frac{1}{4}'' \times 1\frac{3}{4}'' \times \frac{1}{4}''$ yellow metal box with red letters, picture of a guard at an open safe, empty box **6.50**

St. Joseph Cold Tablets, a product of Plough Inc, New York, NY; Memphis, TN, "a palliative aid in relief of simple headache and muscular aches and pains of common cold," 36 tabs, $2\frac{3}{4}'' \times 1\frac{1}{2}'' \times 1''$ light brown and white cardboard box with dark brown letters, full unopened cellophane-wrapped box **6.00**

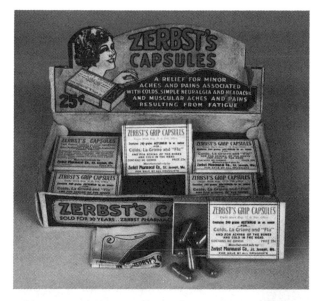

Zerbst's Grips Capsules, mfr only by Zerbst Pharmacal Co, St. Joseph, MO, "for colds, la grippe, and flu, for aching of the bones and cold in the head," 15 tabs, 1½" × 2" × ½" white cardboard box with black and red letters, instruction sheet, full box **5.00**
Display box held 12 boxes, 6¼" × 3⅜" × 1⅜", empty display box **25.00**

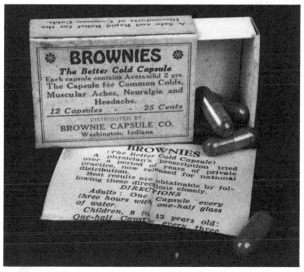

Brownies—The Better Cold Capsule, distr by Brownie Capsule Co, Washington, IN, "the capsule for common colds, muscular aches, neuralgia and headache," 12 caps, 1½" × 2" × ½" white box with red and brown letters, instruction sheet **5.75**

Manazaid Yellow Cold & Anti-pain Tablets, by Manzaid Drug Co, Oberlin, OH, "allays the common cold discomforts of headache, minor muscular aches and pains, neuralgia or periodic discomfort," 18 tabs, 1½" × 2½" × ⅝" white cardboard box with green letters, full unopened box **4.00**

Quinlax Cold Tablets, Vadsco Sales Corp, distr Chicago, New York, San Francisco, "for colds and simple headaches," 24 tabs, 1½" × 2½" white cardboard box with red and green letters, instruction sheet, full box **5.75**

Rehisco Tablets, Walls' Drugs, Indianapolis, IN, "Prescriptions a Specialty," "for the relief of pain and discomfort accompanying colds," 15 tabs, 2¼" × 1" clear glass cylinder with plastic pop-off lid, red and white label with brown letters **5.00**

Rex Cold Tablets, distr by Allied Drug Products Co, Chattanooga, TN, "relief for common colds," 25 tabs, 1" × 2" × ⅝" white

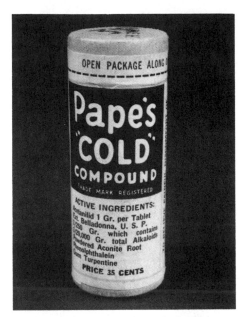

Pape's Cold Compound, made for The Sterling Products, Div of Sterling Drug Inc, Monticello, IL, "to relieve painful discomfort of colds and associated headache," 24 tabs, 2¾" × 1" cylinder with white and maroon letters, full unopened cylinder **8.50**

cardboard box with red and blue letters, full box **3.75**

Special Formula, distr by Kiger's Drug Store, Bowling Green, OH, "for relief of the discomforts of colds such as nasal congestion, headache and neuralgia, muscular aches and pains," 15 caps, 2¾" × 1" × 1" clear glass bottle with white metal lid, light green and white label with dark green letters, full unopened bottle **3.75**

Super Anahist (with Vitamin C), Anahist Co Inc, Yonkers, NY, "an exclusive formula for symptomatic relief of colds in all stages, simple headaches, hay fever," 12 tabs, 2" × ¾" clear glass bottle with blue metal lid, blue and white label with blue and white letters, full unopened bottle **1.00**

Theracin Cold Tablets, Vicks & Theracin are trademarks, Reg. U.S. Pat. Off., Vicks Chemical Co, Div of Richardson-Merrell Inc, Greensboro, NC; New York, NY; Philadelphia, PA, "for fast symptomatic relief of nasal and sinus congestion due to colds and hay fever," 12 tabs, 2" × 1¼" clear green glass bottle with white metal lid in 2½" × 1½" × 1¼" white and green cardboard box with black and white letters, instruction sheet, full unopened box **5.00**

COLD AND COUGH SYRUPS

Extracts from coniferous trees were a main ingredient in cough syrup. In Pfeiffer's Mentholated White Pine and Tar Cough Syrup, chloroform, solid extract of white pine compound, oil of pine tar, ammonium chloride, menthol, glycerin, and honey were added to a simple sugar syrup. Pinex also contained these vital ingredients. Although Lee's Crea-Lyptos For Coughs contained no narcotics, consumers were instructed to sip the syrup every fifteen to twenty minutes allowing it to coat the throat and "hit the spot."

Most of these medications, regardless of whether they contained alcohol, could be given to both children and adults.

Cough Syrup, Moore & Miller Drug Store, Vincennes, IN, "sip 20 drops every 20 or 30 minutes as needed for relief of cough and raw sore throat," 4-fl oz, 5" × 2¼" × 1¼" clear glass bottle with black plastic lid, blue and white label, ½-full bottle **3.00**

Duncan's Exone Cough Syrup, mfr by Standard Medicine Co, St. Louis, MO, "for the relief of coughs due to colds," 4-fl oz, 5⅜" × 2⅛" × 1⅛" clear glass bottle with black metal lid in 6" × 2⅜" × 1¼" red and yellow cardboard box with red letters, ½-full bottle **8.50**

Fortified Cees with GW-3 Cough Medicine, The Norwich Pharmacol Co, Norwich, NY, "for relief of minor bronchial irritation, nasal congestion, and cough due to colds," 3-fl oz, 4¼" × 2" × 1" brown glass bottle with maroon plastic lid, red and white label with black letters, full bottle **4.50**

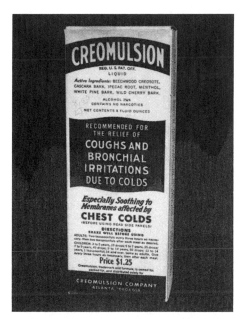

Creomulsion, Creomulsion trademark and formula is owned by, packed for, and distributed by Creomulsion Co, Atlanta, GA, "recommended for the relief of coughs and bronchial irritations due to colds," 8-fl oz, 7¾″ × 2¼″ × 1⅛″ clear glass bottle with black metal lid in 8¼″ × 3⅛″ × 1¾″ tan and black cardboard box with yellow and black letters, full bottle **8.50**

Creo-terpin Compound, prepared solely by Henry K. Wampole & Co Inc, mfg pharmacists, Philadelphia, PA, USA, "a stimulating expectorant for coughs due to colds," 10-fl oz, 7″ × 2¼″ × 1⅝″ clear glass bottle with black plastic lid, white label with green letters, "none genuine without facsimile signature of Henry Wampole," almost-full bottle **6.00**

Gylcaloids, prepared by Koehler Laboratory, Cincinnati, OH, "for coughs due to colds," 16-fl oz, 7¾″ × 3″ × 2″ clear glass bottle with black plastic lid, brown label with black letters, full bottle **9.50**

Hista-pro Cough Syrup, Drugmaster, Inc, St. Louis, MO, "acts to relieve annoying cold symptoms," 4-fl oz, 4½″ × 2″ × 1″ brown glass bottle with white metal lid, brown and yellow label with brown letters, safety seal on lid, full unopened bottle **8.50**

Display: 15″ × 14″ × 10″ brown and yellow cardboard box, holds 36 bottles, picture of woman, display only **15.00**

Laymon's Compound Syrup, made for and packed by World's Products Co, Spencer, IN, USA, "for the relief of coughs due to colds," 2-fl oz, 5⅛″ × 1¾″ × ⅝″ clear glass bottle with black plastic lid in 5¼″ ×

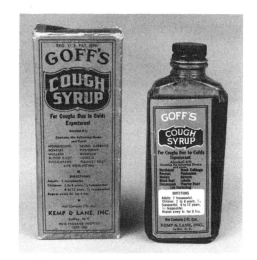

Goff's Cough Syrup, Kemp & Lane Inc, LeRoy, NY, "for coughs due to colds," 2-fl oz, 4½″ × 1¾″ × ⅞″ orange cardboard box with black letters, almost-full bottle **7.00**

Kemp's Balsam, Kemp & Lane Inc, LeRoy, NY, "for coughs due to colds," 2-fl oz, 4½" × 1¾" × ¾" clear glass bottle with blue metal lid in 4¾" × 1⅞" × ⅞" green cardboard box with black and white letters, advertisement for Kemp & Lane products, "new package adopted Sept. 1941," full bottle **7.00**

2" × 1" black and orange cardboard box with black and white letters, ¾-full bottle **8.00**

Penetro Cough Syrup, a product of Plough Inc, New York, NY; Memphis, TN, "expectorant mixture to aid in relief of coughs, husky throat and bronchial irritations due to colds," 3-fl oz, 5" × 2" × ¾" brown glass bottle with orange metal lid in 5⅜" × 2⅛" × 1⅛" orange and white cardboard box with black letters, full bottle **4.00**

6-fl oz, 6¼" × 2½" × ⅞" green glass bottle with orange metal lid in 6⅝" × 2⅝" × 1⅜" orange and white cardboard box with black letters, full bottle **7.00**

Pinex Cough Syrup, distr by Pinex Co Inc, New York, NY, "for coughs and bronchial irritations due to colds," 3-fl oz, 5⅜" × 2" × ¾" clear glass bottle with brown metal lid in 5½" × 2¼" × 1⅛" red and blue cardboard box with white letters, instruction sheet, ⅔-full bottle **4.00**

8-fl oz, 6¾" × 2½" × 1⅛" brown glass bottle with black metal lid, full bottle **7.00**

Super Anahist Cough Syrup, Warner-Lambert Products Div, Morris Plains, NJ, "decongestant with new Triocel, provides 3-way relief of coughs or colds, flu, bronchitis plus the added protection of Vitamin C to help maintain resistance to secondary infection," 7-fl oz, 6¼" × 2½" × 1½" brown glass bottle with black plastic lid in 6½" × 3⅛" × 1½" white cardboard box with orange and blue letters, customer reply form, full bottle **7.00**

Thorexin, the guided Cough Medicine, distr by Gillette Laboratories, Div of the Gillette Co, Chicago, IL, "speeds relief directly to

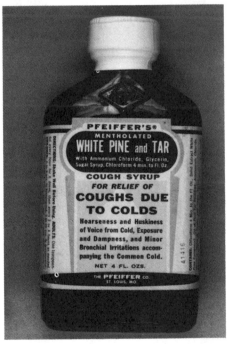

Mentholated White Pine & Tar Cough Syrup, The Pfeiffer Co, St. Louis, MO, "for relief of coughs due to colds, hoarseness and huskiness of voice from cold, exposure and dampness, and minor bronchial irritations accompanying the common cold," 4-fl oz, 4½" × 2" × 1" clear glass bottle with white lid, blue, white, and yellow label with blue and white letters, full bottle **8.50**

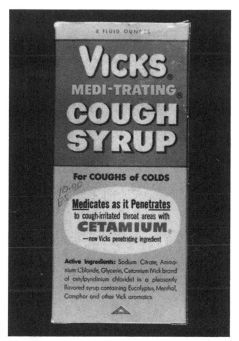

Vicks Cough Syrup, Vick Chemical Co, New York, NY; Greensboro, NC; Philadelphia, PA, for coughs and colds, "mediates as it penetrates," 8-fl oz, 6⅛″ × 2¾″ × 1¼″ clear glass bottle, red, green, and white label with red, green, white, and navy letters, in 7¼″ × 3¼″ × 1⅛″ red, green, and white cardboard box with red, green, navy, and white letters, instruction sheet, full bottle 10.00

the cough control center without narcotics" 4-fl oz, 5″ × 2″ × 1⅛″ clear glass bottle with white plastic lid in 5″ × 2½″ × 1½″ white cardboard box with tan and black letters, instruction sheet, full bottle **10.00**

COUGH DROPS

Penetro Wild Cherry Cough Drops were effective, tasty, and soothing. The Vicks Chemical Company contended that its medicated cough drops made a difference in cough improvement. Estee's low-calorie Dietetic Cough Drops were ideal for the carbohydrate- and calorie-restricted diets. No salt was added, and there were only two calories in each piece.

Dietetic Cough Drops, Dietetic Div Estee Candy Co Inc, New York, NY, USA, 1-oz, 2″ × 3¾″ × ⅝″ white cardboard box with red and blue letters, full unopened box **9.00**

Jessop's Cough Drops, mfr by C. W. Jessop, Connersville, IN, "relieves hoarseness and coughs," 2-oz, 2″ × 3½″ × ½″ white cardboard box with blue letters, empty box **6.50**

Penetro Wild Cherry Cough Drops, Plough Inc, New York, Memphis, "for temporary relief of coughs due to colds," 1⅞″ × 3¼″

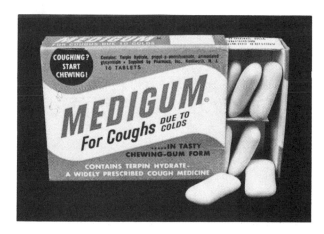

Medigum, supplied by Pharmaco Inc, Kenilworth, NJ, "for coughs due to colds," 16 tabs, 2″ × 2¾″ × ½″ blue and white cardboard box with red and black letters, full box 5.00

× ½" blue and white cardboard box with red, blue, and white letters, full unopened cellophane-wrapped box **5.00**

Vicks Medicated Cough Drops, "Vicks" and "Vaporub" are trademarks Reg. U.S. Pat. Off., Vicks Chemical Co, Div of Richardson-Merrell Inc, Greensboro, NC; New York, NY; Philadelphia, PA, "pleasant-tasting Vicks Cough Drops soothe dry, irritated throat membranes, ease husky, tickling throats, bring fast relief for coughs due to colds," 17-drop 1¾" × 4" × ½" green and blue box with blue and white letters, almost-full cellophane-wrapped box **6.75**

Dental Products

George Washington was renowned for wearing wooden dentures (even though this is a myth!). Many individuals, however, had to put up with ill-fitting dental appliances, despite the number of products available. Diseases of the mouth and gums led to a ready market for pain relievers of all kinds.

DENTURE ADHESIVES AND LINERS

Manufacturers of dental products had a sense of humor when they named products "Chewrite," "Klutch," and "Staze." Denture-eze lasted up to six weeks without reapplication. It also provided relief from messy pastes and powders. Most guarantees on the box alluded to the effectiveness of these products and noted that the consumer could save considerable expense by making fewer visits to the dentist's office.

Brimm's Plasti-Liner, Plasti-Liner Co Inc, Buffalo, NY, "refits and tightens dentures," one liner for one plate, 2-dram vial, Brimm's Tri-Dent Denture Cleaner, in 6½" × ¾" × 1½" navy box with pictures of dentures in red and white **4.00**

*Chewrite, Chewrite Co, Dayton, OH, denture retainer, "holds dental plates firmly in position," ¾-oz, 3¼" × 1½" × 1⅛" clear glass bottle, green, navy, and white label with green, navy, and white letters, unusual cap, full bottle **6.00***

Dentur-Eze Reliner, Dentur-Eze Inc, Seattle, WA, "cushion plastic plate reliner," 6-tablet sample of Dentur-Kleen and wooden applicator for reliner, ¾-oz tube in 1¾" × 2" × 4¼" light blue, pink, and white box with light blue, pink, and white letters, picture of upper plate and tube of reliner, instruction sheet, full tube **5.00**

Denturite Reliner, Denturite Co, Buffalo, NY, mfr by Brimm's Inc, "liquid plastic reliner, enough for 2 plates," two covered plastic dishes of powder, and two glass vials of pink liquid in 4⅝" × 2⅞" × 1" blue, pink, and white box, picture of plates on front, pictured instructions on back **5.75**

Eff-Remin Dentifrice, Goodrich & Love, New York, NY, "effervescent powder for the teeth," 100-gram tin in 3⅛" × 1⅝" × 5⅛" navy blue and white box with navy blue and white letters, instruction sheet and order blank, full tin, mint condition, in original plastic bag **10.00**

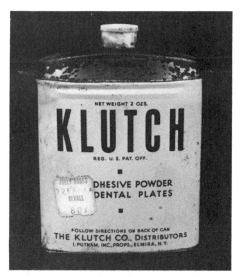

Klutch, The Klutch Co, Distr I. Putnam, Inc, Props, Elmira, NY, "adhesive powder," 2-oz, 4⅛" × 3" × 1" pale blue tin with black letters, full tin **7.00**

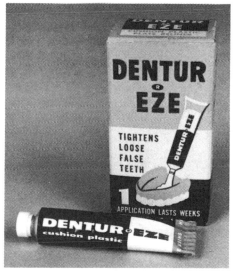

Dentur-Eze, Dentur-Eze Co, Div of Blistex, Inc, Chicago, IL, "cushion plastic reliner, for cold sores, fever blisters, sore cracked lips," ⅓-oz tube with wooden applicator for reliner in 1¾" × 1½" × 3¼" pink, white, and blue box, instruction and advertisement sheet, full foil sample pack of Blistex **5.25**

Kling, American Ferment Co Inc, New York, NY, USA; Carter, Cummings & Co LTD, Windsor, Ontario, CAN, "dental plate adhesive powder," 2-oz tin in 3⅛" × 4¼" × 1¼" tan, light orange, and brown box with brown letters, instruction sheet, full tin, no box top **11.00**

Rexall Denturex, Rexall Drug Co, Los Angeles, Boston, St. Louis, USA, "powder adhesive," 3-oz, 4⅜" × 2½" × 1⅜" light blue, steel gray, and white tin with blue, gray, and white letters, full tin **7.50**

Staze, Staze Labs Inc, Div of Commerce Drug Co Inc, Brooklyn, NY, "denture adhesive with Aquatrol, fluid resistant—holds longer," 1¾-oz tube in 5¾" × 1½" × 1¼" green and white box with black and white letters, instruction sheet, full tube **6.50**

DENTURE CLEANERS

While all denture cleaners claimed to clean false teeth, partial plates, and bridges, only Dent Allure was able to do so in seconds. Other products, such as K.I.K., required at least fifteen to twenty minutes. If a stain was unusually difficult, the recommended time for soaking the dental appliance was several hours or overnight. In addition to cleaning dental appliances, Extar D.C. claimed to stop offensive denture odor and even to remove tartar and eliminate tobacco stains.

Dent Alure, Dentalure Corp, Middletown, OH, "cleans false teeth in seconds," 3-oz, 1¾" × 3½" round brown bottle with red cap, green and white letters, empty bottle **6.50**

Dentur-Kleen, Dentur-eze Inc, Seattle, WA, "dental plate cleaner, no brushing, no measuring, no spilling," six individually cellophane-wrapped tabs in 5" × 1¼" × 1" blue, white, and yellow box, free sample **7.00**

Extar D. C., A J. Parker Co, Winston-Salem, NC; Philadelphia, PA, "denture cleaner,"

8-oz round plastic bottle with cream and red graphics, full bottle **8.00**

K.I.K. (Keep It Kleen), K.I.K. Co, Bethlehem, PA, "brushless denture cleaner, powder," 7-oz, 4" × 2" white and navy round plastic bottle with tin lid, navy letters, full bottle **7.50**

TOOTH AND GUM PAIN RELIEVERS AND ACCESSORIES

Pain remedies for toothaches were usually pellets that the customer would place in the cavity of the tooth or a liquid that could be daubed on painful gums with a cotton swab. The primary ingredient in these medications was oil of cloves.

Gum Balm Liquid Infant's Accessories, Inc, Brooklyn, NY, "relieves toothache, denture pain, teething," 4-fl drams, small brown bottle with red, white, and blue graphics, ¾-full bottle **6.50**

Jiffy Toothache Drops, Hamilton Drug Co, Jersey City, NJ, 1-fl, dram, clear bottle, one toothpick in 1" × 4" × 1" white, red, and black box with white, red, and black letters, small box of cotton pellets for applying drops **5.75**

Sach's Oil of Cloves, Dr. Sachs Laboratories, Chicago, IL, "temporary relief of toothache," ¾" × 2¼" × ¾" brown cork-stoppered bottle with red, tan, and black label and letters, empty bottle **6.00**

Tooth Savers, Pick-A-Dent Corp, San Francisco, CA, "cleans and massages between teeth," 2½" small plastic tool to clean between teeth in blue, black, pink, white clear plastic package with black and white letters, picture of woman's face on front, teeth and "Pick-a-Dent" on back, trial pack of three **4.75**

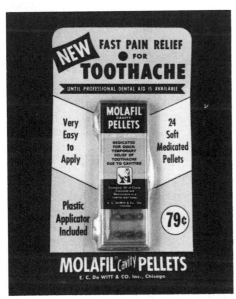

Molafil Cavity Pellets, E. C. DeWitt & Co Inc, Chicago, IL, "relief of toothache due to cavities," 12 individually packed pellets with spatula in 5" × 2" × ¼" slide-top pink and gray packet with pink and black letters, picture of dental chair and drill, full packet 6.75

TOOTHPASTE

Toothpaste gradually replaced most tooth powder in the 1950s. By then, both products contained chlorophyll, stannous fluoride, and durenamel to make teeth cleaner, whiter, and stronger.

Colgate, Colgate-Palmolive Co, Jersey City, NJ, "chlorophyll tooth paste with Gardol," 3¼-oz green and white tube in 6" × 1¼" × 1½" green and white box with red, green, and white letters, full tube **6.00**

Iodent Junior, Iodent Co, Detroit, MI, "stannous fluoride children's toothpaste," 2.75-oz tube, handy roll-up key placed in 6" × 1½" × 1½" red, white, and blue box, three happy kids and toothpaste on front of box, dentist, mother, and daughter on back, almost full tube **10.00**

Ipana, Bristol-Myers Co, New York, NY, "tooth paste with durenamel," 4.6-oz red, white, blue, and gray tube with blue and white letters, almost-full tube **7.50**

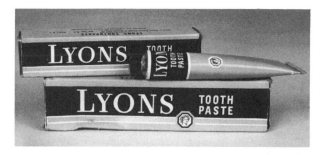

Lyons Toothpaste, The R. L. Watkins Co, Div of Sterling Drug Inc, New York, NY; Rahway, NJ, light and dark blue box, picture of woman's head on top and bottom of box, full 1⅜-oz tube in 5″ × ¾″ × 1⅛″ box (top) **6.75**
Full 2⅞-oz tube in 6¼″ × 1½″ × 1⅛″ box **8.50**

TOOTH POWDER

For many years, tooth powder was simply "tooth powder," whether it was Revelation, Dr. Lyon's, or Pebeco (which was guaranteed to contain the same generous amount of tooth powder despite the new wartime metal-saving container). Pepsodent, Lever Brothers, and Colgate-Palmolive introduced products in the 1950s that contained either irium (purified alkylsulfate) or ammonia, which assured cleaner, whiter teeth.

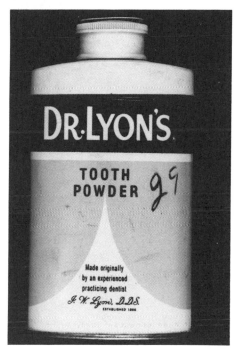

Dr. Lyon's, Glenbrook Labs, Div of Sterling Drug Inc, New York, NY, "originally by J. W. Lyon, DDS, Estab. 1866," tooth powder, 10-oz, 3″ × 5¾″ × 1½″ navy, light blue, and white can with navy, light blue, and white letters, full can **11.00**

Caroid Tooth Powder, Breon Laboratories Inc, subsidiary of Sterling Drug Inc, New York, NY, "cleans and polishes teeth," 2-oz, 5″ × 2½″ × 1⅛″ white and navy tin with light blue, navy, and white letters, ¾-full tin **7.00**

Drucker's Revelation, August E. Drucker Co, San Francisco, CA, USA, "a tooth powder of merit," 1⅛-oz, 3⅛″ × 1⅞″ navy blue and tan cardboard cylinder, navy and white label with navy letters, full cylinder **12.50**

Kontrol, Mark Allen Co, Detroit, MI, "dental stain remover, use before your favorite brand dentifrice, powder," 0.91-oz, 2⅜″ × 1½″ glass vial, plastic pry-off cap, white label with black letters, full vial **3.25**

Pepsodent Tooth Powder, Pepsodent Div, Lever Brothers Co, New York, NY, "contains irium (purified alkylsulfate) for cleaner, white teeth," 2-oz, 3¾″ × 2⅛″ × 1″ pale blue, red, and white horizontal-striped tin with red and white letters, full tin **7.00**

4-oz, 5½″ × 2½″ × 1⅛″ red and white tin with red, black, and white letters, smiling woman on front and back of tin, full tin **12.00**

Peredixo Tooth Powder, American Druggists Syndicate Inc, Laboratories, New

Pebeco, Lehn & Fink Products Corp, Bloomfield, NJ, "tooth powder," 3½-oz, 4¾" × 2¼" round navy and light blue wartime metal-saving container with white graphics, full container **8.00**

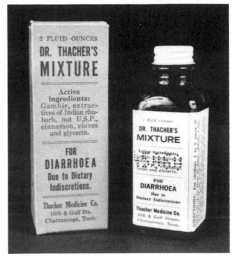

Dr. Thacher's Mixture, Thacher Medicine Co, Chattanooga, TN, "for diarrhoea due to dietary indiscretions," 2-oz, 3½" × 1½" brown bottle in orange box with black letters, ¾-full bottle **8.00**

York, NY, 4½" × 2" × 1½" yellow, red, and black tin with yellow, red, and black letters, slide opening, shaker top, almost-full tin **12.00**

Diarrhea Remedies

Each genuine package of Dr. Thacher's Mixture for "diarrhoea due to dietary indiscretions" bears his "facsimile" signature. Relief is guaranteed without "the attendant evil of constipation." According to Mansfield's Mississippi Cordial, "diarrhea may be serious," and this medication (containing 20 percent ethyl alcohol) "should be taken for no more than two days provided there is no presence of a high fever."

CM, The S. E. Massengill Co, Bristol, TN, "relieves simple diarrhea, upset stomach

nausea, and heartburn," 4-oz, 4⅓" × 2¼" clear glass bottle, white label with blue and white letters **6.00**

Mansfield's Mississippi Cordial, Van Fleet Laboratories, Memphis, TN, "aid in temporary relief of mild diarrhea," 2-oz, 1¾" × 3¾" glass bottle, full bottle **7.50**

Dietary Supplements

Children and adults took dietary supplements to protect against vitamin deficiency. A smiling rosy-cheeked infant's picture depicted the image of perfect health after consuming Berko "Vigortone," a malted milk product that could be prepared either hot or cold.

Chilcott Laboratories manufactured Maltine, which was "a superior concentrate of extract of malted barley with no syrup or sugar other than that derived from cereal." The nutritive components of Maltine included the carbohydrates maltose, dextrose, and dextrin. Maltine's honey-like consistency, because of its heavy concentration of malt, could be diluted with orange juice. Another alternative was to stir the dosage into a cup of milk. Adding some cocoa made this product even more palatable.

Cal-C-Tose "Roche" was used for (1) children who dislike milk, (2) lack of appetite, (3) aid in sleeping, and (4) and the aged, convalescents, and expectant and nursing mothers.

For individuals who simply could not stand the taste or the consistency of such concoctions, some manufacturers made tablets that could be swallowed easily with a glass of water.

Berko "Vigortone," Berko Malted Milk Co Inc, Brooklyn, NY, "chocolate flavored powder, Vitamin A, B1, B2, D etc.," 1-lb, 3″ × 5¾″ round clear glass jar, red-headed baby on label with blue, white, and red graphics glass of malted milk, full jar **6.00**

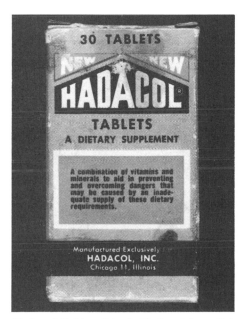

*Hadacol Tablets (New), Hadacol Inc, Chicago, IL, 30 tabs, brown bottle in 1⅞″ × 1⅜″ × 1⅜″ navy blue, gray, and orange box with navy blue and white letters, full bottle **8.50***

*Hadacol, The LeBlanc Corp, Lafayette, LA, dietary supplement, 24-fl oz bottle in 9¼″ × 4¼″ × 2⅛″ light blue, navy blue, and white cardboard box with navy and white letters, full bottle in unopened box **10.00***

Cal-C-Tose, Hoffman-LaRoche Inc, Nutley, NJ, "cocoa and malt flavor, dietary supplement," 12-oz, 3″ × 5⅞″ round tin with pry-off top, yellow, brown, and orange graphics, full tin **12.00**

Maltinc, Chilcott Laboratories, div of The Maltine Co, Morris Plains, NJ, est. 1875, "extract of malted barley," 1-pt, 7¼″ × 2½″ × 3¼″ brown bottle, yellow and black label with black letters, full bottle **12.00**

Min-amin, Nion Corp, Los Angeles, CA, "mineral and vitamin supplement," 5-oz, 2⅜″ × 4¼″ round cardboard container, tan and wine label with wine and black letters, full container **8.00**

Eye Products

Oculine Eye Pads were a welcome way to relieve tired eyes resulting from tension. Many vintage eye products promised to help tired eyes regain their sparkle. Other products, such as "Sight Savers," helped keep eyeglasses impeccably clean. Collectors covet eye-related products because few of these products were ever produced and they are now difficult to locate.

Eye Patches, The Woltra Co Inc, New York City, est. 1923, 2⅝″ × 4″ × 1½″ tan bottle, two black eye patches with strap **3.00**

Ocusol Eye Drops, The Norwich Pharmacal Co, Norwich, NY, "comforts and soothes tired eyes," 1-oz blue stoppered bottle in 4″ × 1¾″ × 1½″ light blue, black, and white box with black and white letters, ¾-full bottle **7.00**

Oph-Thal-O For the Eyes, Edmunds Laboratories, Inc, Detroit, MI, "use 3 times daily or as doctor directs," ½-fl oz brown bottle with stopper in 3¾″ × 1½″ × 1¼″ gold and black box with gold, white, and black letters, ¾-full bottle **8.50**

Rexall's "Eyelo" Eye Lotion, Rexall Drug Co, Los Angeles, Toronto, London, "for eye irritation," 4-fl oz round blue bottle with white plastic eye cup, blue and green label

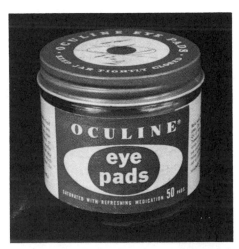

Oculine Eye Pads, Warner-Lambert Products Div, Morris Plains, NJ, "rests, refreshes and soothes tired eyes, medicated eye pads," round glass jar with blue and white label and blue and white metal lid, ⅞-full jar **11.00**

with blue and white letters, full bottle **16.00**

Sight Savers, Dow Corning Corp, Midland, MI, "silicone eyeglass cleaner," ¾-fl oz plastic squeeze bottle, ½-full bottle **3.50**

First-Aid Products

First-aid products went through many permutations from one decade to the next. By the late 1950s, they were so mass-produced that collectors consider very few items from that period "collectible."

ANTISEPTIC POWDERS AND TOPICALS

Alum, boric acid, sulphur, and styptic sticks were universal items in a family's medicine chest. Each had a specific purpose.

The Atco Surgical Supports Company distributed a specially compounded powder to relieve chafing and other skin irritations caused by wearing orthopedic supports and appliances next to the skin. Tyree's Antiseptic Powder was widely used for cuts, abrasions, and nonvenomous insect bites. Non-antiseptic hygienic uses includes: (1) a footwash for tender, tired, and burning feet, (2) a gargle for offensive perspiration, and (3) a douche solution. **Collecting hint:** Look for a variety of products that have multiple or unique uses.

See also First-Aid Products: Liquid Antiseptics.

Atco, Antiseptic Powder, Atco Surgical Supports Co, Cuyahoga Falls, OH, "for chafing and skin irritations caused by orthopedic supports," 2-oz, 3⅛″ × 1¾″ round cardboard cylinder with metal ends, plastic shaker top, olive green, white, and black label and letters, full cylinder **5.75**

B.F.I. Antiseptic Powder, Merck, Sharp & Dohme, Div of Merck & Co, West Point, PA, "for first aid, dressing, and surgical,"

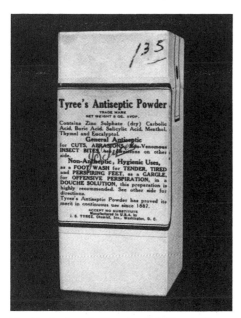

Tyree's Antiseptic Powder, J. S. Tyree, Chemist, Inc, Washington, DC, "general antiseptic," 4-oz, 2″ × 3¾″ × 2″ white box with black, red, and white label, almost-full box **8.00**

7-gram, 2¼″ × 1″ round tin with shaker top and plastic lid, tan, blue, and white label and letters, full tin **5.75**

Domeboro, Powder Packets, Dome Chemicals Inc, New York, NY, "wet dressing for inflammatory conditions of the skin, rash, insect bites, poison ivy, swellings, bruises, or athlete's foot," 12 white 2½″ × 2¼″ paper packets in 3″ × 2⅜″ × 1⅝″ cardboard box, full box **7.00**

Sentinel, Styptic Pencil, Forest City Products Inc, Cleveland, OH, "an aid to coagulation of blood for minor cuts," 6½-gram, 3½″ × ½″ plastic vial with orange, white, and black label and letters, full vial **5.00**

Sulphur, Davis Mfg Co Inc, Knoxville, TN, "sulphur—not U.S.P., not sublimed," 4-oz, 1¾″ × 3¾″ × 1¼″ green and white box with green and white letters, full box **4.00**

EXTERNAL COVERINGS

Johnson & Johnson's Nu Gauze Strip was packed in a brown glass bottle. The 5 percent iodoform salvage-edge strips were *not* sterilized.

Cotton was cotton—or was it?? The Supreme First Aid Company distributed Grade A absorbent cotton that was sterilized after packing. Rexall Quick Puffs were small nonsterile cotton puffs that could simply be plucked from the handy tubular cardboard dispenser. The reusable case was ideal for hosiery, yarn, soap, spools, and other odds and ends, including small tools or cleaning rags, or refilling with cotton balls.

Bandage products changed with the times, and what started as a concern for keeping a wound clean soon included being fashion-conscious. Johnson & Johnson's "Band-Aid" adhesive bandages contained mercurochrome. The United States Plastic Bandage Company distributed fingertip bandages, while the Rexall Drug Company offered extra-large "Quik Bands," which provided special protection for long cuts, scratches, and burns.

Once Band-Aids were made with colorful designs, children no longer were so concerned with minor pain. Tears were replaced with questioning looks as the little ones deliberated over Johnson & Johnson's "Stars 'n Stripes" and "Strips and Spots Charmers."

Absorbent Cotton, Supreme First Aid Co Inc, "sterile cotton," 2-oz, 4¼″ × 1¾″ × 1¾″ red, yellow, white, and tan box with picture of field workers on label, full unopened box **6.00**

Bandage Compresses, Anthes Force Oiler Co, Fort Madison, IA, individual sterilized dressings in 4″ × 2¼″ × ½″ navy and tan pack with navy and tan letters, picture of bandaged hand on back, full pack of one cellophane-wrapped 4″ dressing **6.00**

full pack of four cellophane-wrapped 2″ dressings **6.00**

Band-Aid, Stars 'n Strips, Johnson & Johnson, New Brunswick, NJ, "assorted junior-

Elastoplast Coverlets, Duke Laboratories, Inc, South Norwalk, CT, USA, ¾"-round elastic bandages in 2¾" × 7¼" × 1½" navy and tan box with navy letters, 100 pieces, almost-full **6.50**

Band-Aid Charmers, Johnson & Johnson, New Brunswick, NJ, "assorted adhesive bandages, 9 different designs in box," 2¾" × 3½" × 1¼" white, red, blue, yellow, and green tin with flip-top lid with red and blue letters, empty tin **3.50**

size adhesive bandages, plain assorted colors; ¾" × 3" strips, star assorted colors," in 2¼" × 3½" × 1" white, red, blue, yellow, and green tin with flip-top lid, red and blue letters, almost-empty tin **2.75**

Chiropodists, Johnson & Johnson, New Brunswick, NJ; Chicago, IL, "adhesive felt, soft and flexible, conforms to shape applied to," blue and white mesh cardboard cylinder, metal top and bottom with white labels and red and navy letters, full box of 3' × 7" adhesive felt **10.00**

Curad Tape, Bauer & Black, Chicago, IL, "transparent plastic adhesive tape," ½" ×

160" tape in clear plastic box with hole in the center, red, white, and blue label and letters, full unopened box **3.75**

Fabco, First Aid Bandage Co, Leominster, MA, "self-adhering gauze bandage, does not stick to hair or skin," 1 inch × 5 yards in 1¾" × ⅞" × 1⅛" box, picture on sides of bandage being used on a finger and foot, full sealed box **3.00**

Handi-Tape, Bauer & Black, Chicago, IL, Div of The Kendall Co, Chicago, New York, San Francisco, 16 adhesive tape bandages with "wet pruf" in 1¾" × 1" × 3¾" blue and white tin with black letters, picture of hand with bandage on a finger on front and back of tin **5.00**

Iodosyl Gauze, Nelson, Baker & Co, Detroit, MI, "non-irritant, anti-septic moist dressing," 1 yd in 5¼" × 2" × 2⅛" paper-wrapped box, brown label with silver letters, full unopened box **6.00**

Nu Gauze Strip, Johnson & Johnson, Chicago, IL; New Brunswick, NJ, "non-sterilized gauze strip," 2 inches × 5 yards in 2" × 3¾" round brown bottle, yellow, white, and red label with red letters **8.00**

Parke Dale Absorbent Gauze, Parke, Davis & Co, Detroit, MI, USA, "plain 28/24 mesh gauze," 36 inches × 5 yards in 4½" × 3⅜" × 3½" blue, navy, and white box with red, white, and navy letters, full unopened box **10.00**

FIRST-AID ACCESSORIES AND SUPPLIES

Curity, Bauer, & Black, Div of the Kendall Co, Chicago, IL, "automobile first-aid kit," 7¼" × 5⅜" × 2" red, white, and green tin with red, white, and green letters, empty tin **10.00**

A Friend in Need, Bauer & Black, Div of the Kendall Co, Chicago, New York, Toronto, "First Aid Kit," contents: adhesive tape, surgical gauze, welded-edge gauze bandage, absorbent cotton, ¼-fl oz spirit of ammonia, empty ¼-fl oz bottle of iodine, borated Handi-Tape, and instruction sheet, in 7½″ × 4½″ × 1½″ gold and brown embossed vinyl box **45.00**

Fro-Glow, H. Gloeckler Associates, Inc, New York, NY, "2 in 1 hot pack-cold pack, quick relief for aches and pains," 10¼″ × 8¼″ plastic bag (once contained liquid to heat or freeze for pack use) in 8½″ × 4″ gold and white box, instruction sheet **12.00**

Johnson & Johnson First Aid Packet, Johnson & Johnson, New Brunswick, NJ, box of ten Band-Aids, sterile gauze pads, pack of two Bufferin antacid tablets, tube of antiseptic cream in 5¾″ × 5¾″ × 1½″ red, white, and navy box **10.00**

The Peerless Wood Applicator, B-F-D Division, The Diamond Match Co, New York, NY, 1940, small round wooden medicine applicators 6″ long in 6½″ × 3″ × 2″ green and white box with white letters, almost-full box **7.00**

First Aid Badge, Standard First Aid, sew-on red, green, and white 2½″ round badge, red cross in circle of red and green letters **5.00**

Wire Splint, Anthes Force Oiler Co, Fort Madison, IA, "support for fractures," 4″ × 30″ in 4″ × 2¼″ blue and tan box, picture of man with fractured arm **10.00**

LIQUID ANTISEPTICS

A small cork-stoppered bottle of Math-ol sold for 30¢ in the 1920s. Its healing proponents were distinctly displayed in red and white lettering around the top of the cardboard box: "Tonsilitis Pyorrhea Catarrh Eczema."

Isodine Antiseptic, "the *new* iodine antiseptic," contained an ingredient that changed to a light brown color on the skin and supposedly was visible proof of continuing antiseptic action. It wouldn't stain the skin or any natural fabrics, including silk.

Unbreakable plastic squeeze bottles containing antiseptics began to appear in the 1940s. Abbott Laboratories' Tronolen Lotion relieved pain and itching. Rexall's Kant Sting was a nonstinging antiseptic that killed germs— ideal for taking on picnics or to the beach. Tronolen was guaranteed not to stain modern bathing suits.

The 1960s witnessed the introduction of medications in tubes, including Medi-Quick and Bactine.

Chloraide, Farmaide Products Co, Lincoln, NE, "general sanitation and antiseptic use," 1-qt round brown rubber-cork bottle in 4″ × 10″ × 4″ tan, navy, and green box with tan and navy letters, full bottle **6.00**

Credosol, L. Perrigo Co, Allegan, MI, "disinfectant antiseptic," 4-fl oz clear glass bottle in 2¼″ × 1¼″ × 6¼″ tan and navy box with white and navy letters, no top on box, almost-full bottle **8.50**

Isodine Antiseptic, Isodine Pharmacol Corp, Dover, DE, "the new iodine antiseptic," ½-fl oz brown glass bottle with glass applicator, in 3⅛″ × ⅞″ × 1⅛″ tan, brown, and white box with brown letters, 1956 instruction sheet, full bottle **3.00**

Math-ol, Math-ol Inflammacine Co Inc, mfg chemists, Rochester, NY, "antiseptic and germicide," round clear bottle with cork stopper in 2¼" × 6" × 2¼" tan and red box with green and tan letters, no top on box, instruction sheet, almost-full bottle **11.00**

Medi-quick, Lehn & Fink Products Corp, Bloomfield, NJ, "medicated cream, relieves pain, helps prevent infection, speeds healing, minor skin irritations," 1½-oz tube in 5¾" × 1½" × 1¼" red, white, and blue box with red, white, and black letters, instruction sheet, almost-full tube **6.75**

Mercurochrome, L. Perrigo Co, Allegan, MI, "does not injure tissue," 1-oz bottle with glass applicator, 3⅜" × 1¼" × ⅞" navy, black, and white label with navy and white letters, full bottle **3.50**

Reliable Brand, McCormick & Co, Baltimore, MD, "solution of hydrogen peroxide," 4-oz, 4½" × 1½" round brown glass bottle, navy, gray, and white label with navy, white, red, and gray letters, copyright 1932, empty bottle **8.75**

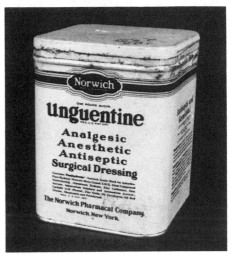

Unguentine, The Norwich Pharmacal Co, Norwich, NY, "analgesic, anesthetic, surgical dressing, relieves pain, promotes healing," 1-lb, 3" × 4" × 3" yellow, black, and red tin with black letters, full tin **11.00**

Rexall Kant Sting, Rexall Drug Co, Los Angeles, St. Louis, Toronto, "antiseptic, kills germs, cleans wound," 4-fl oz, 5¼" × 2½" × 1¼" light green plastic squeeze bottle with white letters, almost-full bottle **9.00**

Tronolen Lotion, Abbott Laboratories, North Chicago, IL, "temporary pain and itching, sunburn, insect bites, other minor skin irritations," 75-ml, 4¼" × 2" × 1" light blue and green squeeze bottle, full bottle **3.25**

Foot Products

The name "Dr. Scholl" has always been and still is synonymous with foot-products. Callous Salve, Foot Balm, Foot Powder (both in cardboard and tin), and Moleskin Foot Plaster were displayed prominently in a case designed exclusively for his products. Outgro (relieves pain of ingrown nails), Off-Ezy (corn and callus remover), and Jiffy One-Night Corn Salve (a tiny tin with smiling feet is included in the box) diverted a person's discomfort for a few minutes with a bit of humor.

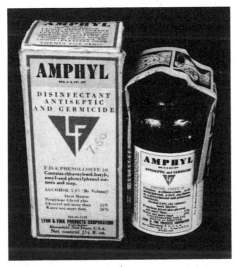

Amphyl, Lehn & Fink Products Corp, Bloomfield, NJ, "disinfectant, antiseptic and germicide," 2½-fl oz, round, embossed clear glass bottle in 2" × 4⅜" × 2" white, red, and tan box with red and black letters, instruction sheet, almost-full bottle **8.00**

FOOT MEDICATIONS, PADS, AND PLASTERS

Foot medications often relieved athlete's foot as well as tired and tender sweating feet. Nyal Foot Bath Tablets also relieved corns, bunions, and frostbite. Derma-Kylbac was the proven treatment for athlete's foot. Applications of this treatment were also beneficial for fungus infections on hands and feet.

Advicin Cream, Schering Corp, Bloomfield, NJ, "antifungal cream for athlete's foot," 30-gram aluminum tube in 5″ × 1″ × 1½″ wine and white box with wine and white letters, almost-full tube **6.50**

Blue Jay Callus Plasters, Blue-Jay Products, Div of the Kendall Co, Chicago, "felt pads relieve pressure pain and shoe rub, medication gently loosens callus, wet-pruf adhesive tabs hold medication firmly in place, even in bath," three callus plasters in 2¾″ × 3½″ × ½″ green, navy, white, and yellow box with green, black, and white letters, picture of callus plaster on back, full pack **7.00**

Little Joe Ointment, Bell Chemical Co, Chicago, IL, "removes corns and callouses," ½-oz, 1⅜″ × 1½″ round milk-glass jar with white metal lid, navy and yellow label with black and white letters, picture of smiling face, full bottle **13.00**

Cold Spot Corn Relief, The Penslar Co Inc, Detroit, MI, "softens corns for removal," 7-cc octagonal brown bottle with glass applicator cap, four felt pads, in 1¾″ × 2⅝″ × 1⅛″ dark green, gray, and white box with red, green, and white letters, picture of mountains and pine trees, empty bottle **7.00**

Derma-Kylbac, Medical Arts Supply Co Inc, Huntington, WV, "The Proven Treatment" for athlete's foot, 4-fl oz round brown bottle in 5″ × 2″ × 2″ green, olive, and black box with black and white letters, picture of a hand touching a foot, almost-full bottle **8.75**

Dr. Scholl's Callous Salve, The Scholl Mfg Co, Chicago, New York, Toronto, London, Paris, "removes callouses and hard, thickened skin on feet," ¼-oz aluminum tube, two zinc pads, 1⅝″ × ¾″ × 3⅜″ in yellow and light blue box with black and red letters, instruction sheet, Good Housekeeping Guarantee, full box **6.00**

Dr. Scholl's Foot Balm, The Scholl Mfg Co Inc, Chicago, New York, Toronto, London, "soothes, rests, and refreshes tender, tired, sensitive feet," 1½-oz, 2¼″ × 2″ round milk glass jar, yellow, red, and light blue label with black and white letters, "Dr. Scholl's" written on metal cap, copyright 1948, **7.00**

3½-oz milk glass jar with yellow and light blue label and black letters, ½-full jar **8.75**

Eagle's Antiseptic, Eagle Chemical Co, Chattanooga, TN, "for discomfort of ringworm of the hands and feet," 5¼″ × 2¼″ round spray can with black, red, and white label and black and white letters, picture of a foot on front, almost-empty can **5.00**

Furaspor Cream, Eaton Laboratories, Div of The Norwich Pharmacol Co, Norwich, NY, "for topical fungicide, sporicide, and bactericide ringworm of the feet, scalp, and skin," 28-gram round milk glass jar with metal cap in 1¾″ × 1¾″ × 2¼″ black, white, and olive box with black and white letters, March 1961, instruction sheet for pharmacists, almost-empty jar **5.75**

Hanson's Magic Corn Salve, W. T. Hanson Co, Schenectady, NY, since 1884,

Reese's Bunion Reliever, The Reese Chemical Co, Cleveland, OH, "reliever salve soothes surface inflammation, pads relieve shoe pressure," 45-gram tube of reliever and six adhesive bunion pads in 2¾" × 2" × 1" yellow, black, and red box with red letters, picture of an old farmer, axe in hand, sore foot upon tree stump, and a crow telling him, "Don't cut off your toe," almost-full tube **8.00**

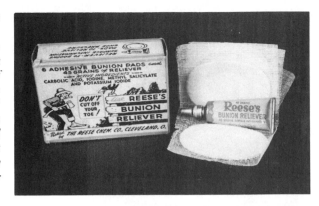

Brockville, ONT, "stops pain quickly, often removes corns in one night," ⅕-oz 1½" × 1½" × 1" round orange wooden box, instruction sheet, full box **12.00**

Howell's Chex, The Howell Co, New Orleans, LA, "antiseptic, deodorant, fungicide, relieves itching, checks fungus of athlete's foot and other forms of parasitic skin eruptions and irritations," 1-fl oz, 3½" × 1½" × ¾" brown glass bottle with applicator cap, blue, white, and yellow label with blue and white letters, almost-full bottle **6.75**

Ideal Wart, Corn, and Callus Remover, Ideal Laboratories, Grand Rapids, MI, "salve to soften warts, corns, and calluses for removal," ½-oz, 2" × 1½" round green glass bottle, red, white, and blue label with blue and white letters, full bottle **4.00**

Jiffy One Night Corn Salve, Kohler Mfg Co, New York, NY, "treats corns and callouses," adhesive tape in cellophane wrap, corn pad, wooden applicator stick for salve, in 2⅝" × ¾" × ⅜" dark blue, orange, and white box, stars on front, picture of two "happy face" feet on back, no salve left, instruction/advertising sheet, **5.00**

Keyes Bunion Pads and Plasters, The Keyes Mfg Co, Cincinnati, OH, "plasters relieve pain, pads stop shoe pressure," four medicated plasters and adhesive plaster felt pads in 4¾" × 4½" × ¼" light green, dark blue, and white box with white and dark blue letters, pictures of feet on back and front, cellophane window in front show-

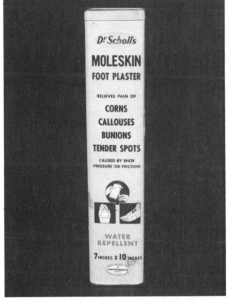

Dr. Scholl's Moleskin Foot Plaster, The Scholl Mfg Co Inc, Chicago, New York, Los Angeles, Toronto, London, "relieves pain of corns, bunions, callouses, tender spots caused by shoe pressure or friction, water repellent," 7" × 10" piece of moleskin plaster in 8" × ¼" × 1¾" yellow, blue, and white tin with black, blue, and red letters, Good Housekeeping Guarantee, copyright 1959 **12.00**

ing pads and plasters, copyright 1939, "Good Housekeeping" Bureau Tested and Approved oval sign, full package **6.75**

Keyes Soft Corn Pads and Plasters, The Keyes Mfg Co, Cincinnati, OH, "pads relieve pain, plasters remove corns," 16 medicated plasters and 12 adhesive plaster felt pads in 7½″ × 3¼″ × ¼″ in light green, dark blue, and white package with white and dark blue letters, pictures on back and front of foot and pads, cellophane window in front shows pads and plasters, copyright 1939, "Good Housekeeping" Bureau Tested and Approved oval sign, full package **5.00**

Mosco, Moss Chemical Co Inc, Rochester, NY, USA, "hard corn and callous remover" ¼-oz, 1¼″ × 1¼″ milk glass bottle with red and white metal cap, gold, yellow, and red label with red, black, and white letters, full bottle **8.00**

½-oz, 1¼″ × 1½″ milk glass bottle, no label, ¾-full bottle **6.25**

Nyal Foot Bath Tablets, Nyal Co, Detroit, MI, "relieves tired, aching, tender, swollen feet, corns, bunions, callous, frost bites, chilblains," 35 foot-shaped tabs, 2¾″ × 2″ × 1″ orange, tan, and white slide-top box with black letters, Nyal Products Advertis-

ing Sheet, adopted 1916, almost-full box **6.00**

Off-Ezy with Benzocaine, Commerce Drug Co Inc, Brooklyn, NY, "relieves the pain and removes the corn or callous promptly," round brown glass bottle, glass applicator cap in 3½″ × 1″ × 1″ red, white, and yellow box with black and white letters, picture of foot with a corn on toe, ½-full bottle **3.00**

Outgro, Whitehall Laboratories, Inc, New York, NY, "relieves pain of ingrown nails," 2½-fl drams, octagonal glass bottle, glass applicator under top, 3½″ × 1″ × 1″ yellow, dark green, and white box with dark green and white letters, advertising and instruction sheet, full bottle **7.50**

Phy-Tox Antiseptic Ointment, Rae Chemical Co, Cincinnati, OH, "treatment of athlete's foot and ringworm of the body, exclusive of the nails and hairy portions," 175-gram round milk glass jar in 2⅛″ × 1½″ × 1½″ black and white box with black and white letters, full jar **8.50**

FOOT POWDERS

Advicin Antifungal Powder, Schering Corp, Bloomfield, NJ, "athlete's foot discomfort relief," 1¼-oz, 4½″ × 1¼″ cardboard cylinder with wine and tan label and letters, almost-full cylinder **3.50**

2-oz, 5″ × 1¼″ round tin, full tin **5.00**

Decillin Powder, The Penslar Co Inc, New York, NY, "relieves fungus infections of the skin, as athlete's foot and other types of surface ringworm," 3-oz, 4″ × 2½″ tan, wine, and white cardboard cylinder with white and wine letters, metal shaker top, metal bottom, almost-full cylinder **5.00**

Desenex Powder, WTS-Pharmacraft, Div of Wallace & Tiernan Inc, Rochester, NY, USA, "for athlete's foot and ringworm of the body," ¼-oz, 3″ × 1″ round yellow and wine tin with yellow and wine letters, ½-full tin **10.00**

½-oz, 4″ × 1¾″ round yellow and wine tin, full tin **6.75**

Dr. Scholl's Foot Powder, The Scholl Mfg Co Inc, Chicago, New York, Toronto, Paris,

Zanol Foot Balm, The Zanol Products Co, Cincinnati, OH; New York, Paris, "cools and refreshes, deodorizes, helps check excessive perspiration," 3-oz, 2¾″ × 2″ round blue glass jar with light blue metal cap, light blue and dark blue label and letters, almost-empty jar **7.00**

London, "soothing, refreshing, neutralizes foot odors," 3½-oz, 1¾ × 5" round black, yellow, white, and light blue tin with black letters, picture of powder being used on a foot and in a shoe on back of tin, full tin **7.00**

3¼-oz, 4½" × 1¾" yellow, light blue, and black cardboard cylinder with black letters, no top, almost-empty cylinder **6.50**

Gets-It Foot Powder, Plough, Inc, New York, NY; Memphis, TN; Los Angeles, CA, "medicated antiseptic, fungicidal, soothing relief for tired, hot feet, neutralizes foot odors, preventing athlete's foot," 2¼-oz, 4¾" × 1¾" green, yellow, and white round tin with green, yellow, and white letters, almost-full tin **9.00**

Jiffy Foot Powder, Jiffy Remedies Co, Downers Grove, IL, "comforting, soothing, relief of excessive sweating and undue friction," 1⅞-oz cardboard cylinder with light pink label and navy letters, metal shaker top, pry-open bottom, full cylinder **8.00**

Quinsana Powder, The Mennen Co, Newark, NJ; Toronto, Ontario, CAN, "for fungus infection of the feet," 4⅓-oz, 5" × 1¾"

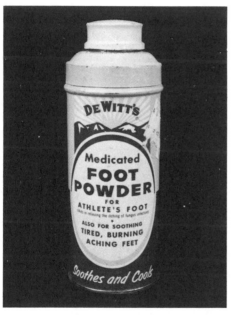

DeWitt's Foot Powder, E. C. DeWitt & Co Inc, Chicago, IL, "temporary easing of hot, tired, burning feet, borated and sanitary," 2½-oz, 4½" × 1¾" yellow, green, and white round tin with green and white letters, full tin **7.00**

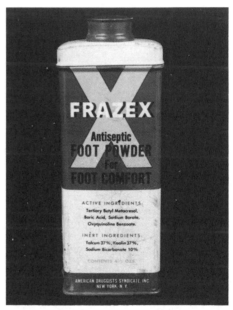

Frazex Powder, American Druggists Syndicate, Inc, New York, NY, "antiseptic foot powder for foot comfort," 4½-oz, 6" × 2¼" × 1¼" blue, cream, and yellow tin with blue, cream, black, and yellow letters, "X" on front and back, almost-full tin **6.00**

Newton's Foot Relief, Paul D Newton & Co, Newark, NY, "a scientific preparation for the relief of tired, aching feet," 4" × 1" × 1" white box with black letters on tan label, no size listed, full unopened box **7.50**

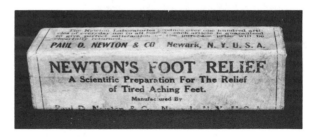

TIZ Foot Powder, The Larned Corp, Distr, formerly Wyeth Chemical Co, Jersey City, NJ, USA, "soothes, reduces foot odors," 2-oz, 4½" × 1½" yellow and black cardboard cylinder with black letters, metal top and pry-open bottom, almost-full cylinder **10.00**

× 1¾" two-tone light blue and white tin with navy and white letters, full tin **6.00**

Sopronol Powder, Wyeth Laboratories, Inc, Philadelphia, PA, "athlete's foot powder," 2-oz tan and cream metal cylinder with navy label and navy letters, almost-full cylinder **6.00**

Timofax Foot Powder, Burroughs Wellcome and Co Inc, Tuckahoe, NY, "for prevention and treatment of the fungus infection of the skin, athlete's foot," 1½-oz, 1⅞" × 4¼" pale blue metal cylinder, wine-color cap, white and pale blue label with wine letters, picture of a unicorn on front, almost-full cylinder **8.00**

Herbal Remedies

Initial Line, Murray & Nickell, Allaire-Woodward & Company, and the S. B. Penick Companies were some of the largest manufacturers of herbs used for herbal remedies. Smaller, regional com-

panies included the Stream Drug Mills and the Huber & Fuhrman Drug Mills, both of Fond du Lac, Wisconsin.

Herbs were often packed in small, square cardboard boxes and were guaranteed under the Food and Drugs Act of June 30, 1906, Serial Number 1859. Murray & Nickell incorporated the following information on each package of herbs:

Stramonium Leaves

Common Name: Thorn Apple, Jamestown Weed, Apple of Peru, Stinkweed, Devil's Apple.

Scientific Name: Stechapfel

Properties: In overdoses, a narcotic poison.
In medicinal doses useful in mania epilepsy, and allays rheumatic and syphilitic pains.
Dose 2 to 5 grains.

Herbs were mixed to achieve the desired herbal remedy for a specific ailment. A wine glass was the common measure when consuming an infusion of herbs mixed with one pint of water. Some liquids were to be taken warm, some at room temperature, and some cool. Each herb had various healing properties, including cures for flatulence, jaundice, worms, and catarrh. Some acted as an antispasmodic, tonic, laxative, or diuretic. Herbs were also used to make a poultice for bruises or inflammations.

Collecting hint: Purchase only packages of herbs that do not have any holes or other signs of insect damage. Always put the herbs in plastic bags in the freezer for at least a week to kill any bugs or mites.

Acacia Gum, Penick S. B. Penick & Co, New York, Chicago, "soothing for inflamed tissue," 1-lb, 5" × 3" × 3" gold metal container with blue and white label and black letters, full container **11.00**

Buckthorn Bark, Allaire-Woodward & Co, Peoria, IL, "tonic, laxative," 1″ × 2¼″ × 2¼″ brown cardboard box with black letters, full box **4.50**

Catechu Gum, S. B. Penick & Co, New York, Chicago, "powerful astringent, gargle," 1-lb, 5″ × 3″ × 3″ gold metal container, yellow and brown label with yellow and brown letters, full container **13.00**

Chestnut Leaves, S. B. Penick & Co, Crude Drugs, New York, NY; Asheville, NC: Chicago, IL; Jersey City, NJ, "made into tea to be used for whooping cough," 1-oz, 1½″ × 2½″ × 2½″ gray, white, and blue cardboard box with black and blue letters, full box **6.00**

Fennel Seed N. F., S. B. Penick & Co, New York, Chicago, "carminative, calmative, decongestant," ¼-lb, 3½″ × 2½″ × 2½″ gold metal container, yellow and brown

Pipsissewa Herb, Murray & Nickell Mfg Co, Chicago, USA, "astringent, diuretic, tonic," 2¼″ × 2⅛″ × ⅞″ brown cardboard box with black letters, full box 4.50

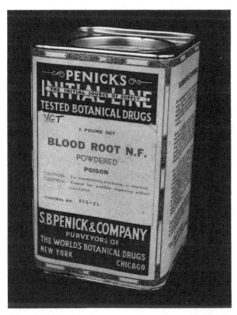

Blood Root N. F., S. B. Penick & Co, New York, Chicago, "expectorant, emetic, stimulant, cathartic, antiseptic," 1-lb, 6″ × 3⅓″ × 3½″ gold metal container, brown and yellow label with red, brown, and yellow letters, full container 12.00

label with yellow and brown letters, ½-full container **8.00**

Flaxseed Meal, Distr by National Package Drugs Inc, St. Louis, MO, "for poultices," 4-oz, 4¼″ × 2¼″ cardboard cylinder, yellow and brown label with brown letters, full unopened cylinder **6.00**

Ginger Root Jamaica, S. B. Penick & Co, New York, Chicago, "soothe indigestion and take the wind out of flatulence," ¼-lb, 3½″ × 2½″ × 2½″ gold metal container, blue and white label with black letters, full container **7.00**

Henna Powder, packaged by Purepac Corp, New York, NY; Chicago, IL; Los Angeles, CA, "dyes, astringent, stimulant," 2-oz, 2″ × 2½″ × 1¾″ pink and maroon metal box with maroon and white letters, full box **6.50**

Juniper Berries N.F., S. B. Penick & Co, New York and Chicago, "expectorant, emetic, stimulant, cathartic, antiseptic," 1-lb 6″ × 3½″ × 3½″ gold metal container, brown and yellow label with red, brown, and yellow letters, full container **12.00**

Mullein Leaves, Murray & Nickell Mfg Co, Chicago, "demulcent, diuretic and anodyne, useful in catarrh, coughs, diarrhea, and dysentery," 2¼″ × 2⅛″ × ⅞″ brown cardboard box with black letters, guaran-

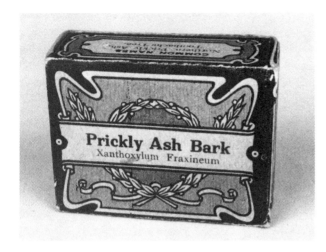

Prickly Ash Bark, Huber & Fuhrman Drug Mills, Fond du Lac, WI, "tonic alterative sialagogue, stimulant," 2" × 2½" × 1" blue and brown cardboard box with blue letters, "guaranteed under the Pure Food & Drug Act, June 30, 1906," full box **5.75**

teed under the Food and Drug Act, June 30, 1906, full box **4.75**

Psyllium Seed, packaged by Purepac Corp, New York, NY; Chicago, IL; Los Angeles, CA, laxative, 1-lb, 5" × 3¾" × 2½" pink and maroon metal box with green letters, full box **8.00**

Pyrethrum Powder, S. B. Penick & Co., New York, Chicago, "insecticide used against pests and certain sucking insects such as aphids which are in need of contact washes," 1-lb, 6" × 4" × 4" metal container, yellow and brown label with brown letters, almost-empty container **8.50**

Sassafras, S. B. Penick & Co Inc, Crude Drugs, New York, NY, USA; Asheville, NC; Chicago, IL; Weehawken, NJ, "effective remedy for skin wounds," 1-oz, 2⅝" × 2¾" × 1½" white, gray, and blue cardboard box with black and blue letters, full box **6.00**

Stramonium Leaves, Murray & Nickell Mfg Co, Chicago, USA, "in overdoses a narcotic poison, in medicinal doses useful in mania epilepsy and allays rheumatic and syphilitic pains," 2¼" × 2¼" × ¾" yellow cardboard box with black letters, full box **4.25**

Summer Savory, put up by Allaire-Woodward & Co, Peoria, IL, "carminative useful in flatulent colic," 2¼" × 2¼" × 1" brown cardboard box with black letters, full box **4.50**

Vervian Root, Steam Drug Mills, Fond du Lac, WI, "astringent, antispasmodic," 1-oz, 1¾" × 3⅝" × ¾" blue paper-wrapped package with black letters, full package **4.50**

Wormwood Leaves, Murray & Nickell Mfg Co, Chicago, "anthelmintic, tonic, narcotic," ⅞" × 2⅛" × 2⅛" brown cardboard box with black letters, full box **4.50**

Hospital and Surgical Appliances

Bedpans have undergone various design changes in the last fifty years, as have urinals and catheters. These items are still inexpensive and readily available. And no home would be without a hot water bottle for emergency pain!

Defender Crutch Tips and the Sheppard Blood-Taking Tube are among collectibles that are more difficult to locate.

Bed pan and urinal, white porcelain-coated metal, no lid, 12" × 18" from end to spout **12.00**

Catheters, Miller Rubber, Div of the B. F. Goodrich Co, Akron, OH, USA, red rubber catheters, closed tip, depressed "eye", 16" length to funnel end, 2⅛″ × ¾″ × 16¾″ navy and white box with navy and white letters **2.50 each, 3 for 7.00**

Clinitest, Ames Co Inc, Elkhart, IN, USA, glass test tubes, box of six clear glass 2¾″ tubes in 4¼″ × 3″ × ¾″ tan and navy box with navy letters, two left in box **8.00**

Combination Attachment, Daval Inc, Daval Rubber Co, Providence, RI, "converts water bottle to fountain syringe," 5¾″ × 5¾″ × 1¼″ blue and white box with blue letters, empty box **7.00**

Davol-Davol Rubber Co, Providence, RI, assortment of syringe fillings, 6¼″ × 8¼″ × 1¼″ orange, yellow, blue, and black box with black letters, almost empty **3.00**

Defender Crutch Tips, Rexall Drug Co, Los Angeles, Boston, St. Louis, USA; Toronto, CAN, Size 16 rubber tips, twelve black tips, 2⅝″ × 3½″ × 1¾″ tan box with white and yellow label and blue and yellow letters, each tip 1.50, full box of 12 **18.00**

Dex Co, Ideal Instruments & Mfg Co, Chicago, IL, one boxed intravenous set (ID 165), 5½′-long rubber tube with metal end, packaged needle, rubber open-

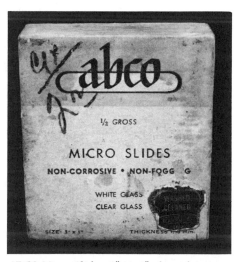

ABCO Micro Slides, 3″ × 1″ clear glass noncorrosive, nonfogging slides, ½ gross, 3¼″ × 3¾″ × 1″ yellow, white, and brown box, almost-full box **12.00**

ended bulb at other end, in 3¼″ × 6½″ × 1½″ green and tan box with black letters **10.00**

B. F. Goodrich Catheters, The B. F. Goodrich Co, Akron, OH, USA, one red catheter 16″-long depressed eye, surgical quality, funnel end closed tip, in 2¼″ × ¾″ × 16¾″ green and white box with green and white letters **5.75**

Hot Water Bottle with Hose, Davidson Red Rubber, black plastic end **8.00**

Hygienic Gloves, Lindfelt Glove Mfg Co, Des Moines, IA, "for protection of sensitive hands," one pair ladies, small size, cotton, cellophane-wrapped gloves, information sheet **8.50**

Index Brand, Johnson & Johnson, New Brunswick, NJ, "disposable enema, single use," 4½″-long plastic compact tube with syringe tip in 1¼″ × 4½″ × 1″ blue and white box with blue letters **6.75**

Jones Specialized Pus Basin, The Jones Metal Products Co, West Lafayette, OH, hospital surgical ware, white enamel with blue trim, 7½″ × 3½″ × 1½″ kidney-shaped basin #8, blue, gold, black, and white label **10.00**

Laverna Compound, Winthrop Laboratories, Div of Sterling Drug Inc, New York, NY, "disposable enema kit," 6-oz clear plastic accordion-type bottle, hose and syringe in 5″ × 2¾″ × 2¾″ light blue, dark blue, and white box with blue letters **11.00**

Safti Flask, Cutter Laboratories, Berkeley, CA, "fractionally distilled water I.V. Bottle," 2 liter, 4¼″ × 4¼″ × 13½″ clear glass bottle, embossed measurements, metal hook for hanging on bottom of bottle, rounded at top, square at bottom **135.00**

The Sheppard Blood-Taking Tube, The Scientific Glass Instrument Co Inc, Northfield, NJ, box of 12, clear glass and rubber blood-taking tubes, individually wrapped in tissue paper, in 6½″ × 2″ × 3⅛″ tan and brown box, picture of blood-taking tube on top, 11 left in box **65.00**

Standard Surgeon's Gloves, The Seemless Rubber Co, New Haven, CT, smooth latex, size 6, in 6″ × 3½″ × 1¼″ yellow and

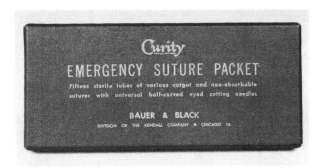

Curity Suture Packet, Bauer & Black, Div of The Kendall Co, Chicago, IL, "emergency suture packet, 15 sterile tubes of various cat gut and nonabsorbable sutures with universal half-curved, eyed cutting needles," sutures encased in glass tubes with sterile fluid, 7¼" × 3¼" × ¾" black case, six tubes in case **20.00**

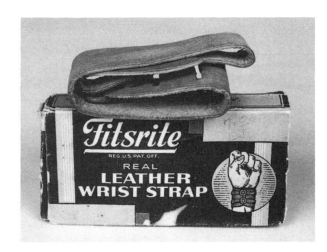

Fitsrite Wrist Strap, Fitsrite Products Co, New York City, USA, support for sprains, strains, weak wrists, and all sports, leather wrist strap in 5" × 2½" × 1" navy and orange box with navy, orange, and white letters, an arm pictured wearing wrist strap on front and back of box, one end of box missing **7.00**

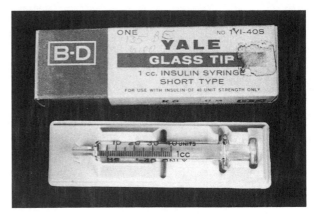

Yale, Becton, Dickinson & Co, Rutherford, NJ, 1-cc, insulin syringe, glass tip, short type, "for use with insulin of 40-unit strength only," in plastic holder, 4⅛" × 1¼" × ¾" tan and orange box with tan and orange letters **6.00**

brown box with yellow and brown letters, one pair **8.00**

Water Bottle, Abbott Laboratories, 100-ml, 3¾" × 8¾" round clear glass bottle with rubber stopper, embossed measurements, can be hung upside down, no attachments on bottle **9.00**

Infant and Children Products

Most drugstores carried a basic line of products for infants and children, including layette items, vitamins, and various teething rings.

Usually, the more varied the infant section, the more affluent the drugstore. Certain sections were devoted exclusively to cough and cold products, laxatives, and feeding accessories. Not only was there a general heading entitled "Baby Needs," but subheadings designated more specific sections, such as skin remedies and baby books.

INFANT AND CHILDREN COUGH AND COLD PRODUCTS

Most children's cough syrups were flavored with cherry, orange, or honey. Kiddie-Kof Suckers were promoted as "a medicine, *not* a candy." They were to be dissolved slowly in the mouth and *never* chewed. Sal-Payne was a children's analgesic compound that also contained caffeine. Nokof Children's Cough Syrup contained 1 percent alcohol. Cough syrup companies strongly advocated discontinuing any of these products if a high fever or cold symptoms persisted for more than seven days.

Children's Mild Musterole, The Musterole Co, Cleveland, OH, "congestion, pain, skin rub," 1⅝" × 2¼" round milk glass jar with embossed metal cap, green and white label with red, green, and white letters, almost-empty jar **8.00**

Bronchola, Bronchola Co, Peoria, IL, "children's cough syrup," 4-fl oz, 4½″ × 1¾″ round clear glass bottle, ivory painted-on label and letters, wheat arch, small mortar and pestle on front of bottle, full bottle **8.00**

Chest Rub Stick, Johnson & Johnson, New Brunswick, NJ, "will not burn or sting," for pains, congestion, coughs, and head stuffiness, 2.3-oz, 3¾″ × 2″ round clear glass jar, pale blue and white label with red, black, and blue letters, full jar **4.00**

Creomulsion Cough Syrup, Creomulsion Co, Atlanta, GA, "children's flavored cough syrup," 4-fl oz, 1½″ × 2½″ × 5″ clear glass bottle in pink, blue, and white box with black and white letters, picture of smiling girl and boy, full bottle **8.00**

Kiddie-Kof Suckers, Sharp & Shearer, Reading, PA, "medicinal product for coughs due to the common cold," six suckers in 3¾″ × 4″ × 1″ pink, blue, and white box

with blue and white letters, full unopened cellophane-wrapped box **7.00**

Sal-Payne, Sal-Payne Corp, Dayton, OH, USA, "for mild headache, cold symptoms," children's size capsules in 1⅞″ × ⅜″ × ¾″ navy, orange, and white tin box, full slide top, orange and white letters, seven capsules **7.00**

Tycolene Cold Syrup, The Pfeiffer Co, St. Louis, MO, "children's multiple action cold syrup," 4-fl oz, 2½″ × 1½″ × 4¾″ clear glass bottle in navy, yellow, and white box with navy letters, silhouette of a child, full bottle **8.00**

INFANT AND CHILDREN FEEDING ACCESSORIES

Three Capson Baby Bottle Sterilizers were used by Dr. Dafoe in his care of the famous Dionne quintuplets of Canada in the 1930s. The effectiveness of the Capson sterilizer was attributed to the live steam used to sterilize the bottles. Once baby was able to eat pureed food or toddler snacks, the sterilizer could be used to accommodate three quart-size canning jars when it was time to preserve nature's bounty.

The Kayware baby cup was available in the two standard baby colors—pink and blue. Made in one piece from Luxtrex, "The Royal Plastic," this practically spillproof baby cup could be sterilized in boiling water.

Dr. Drake's Glessco, The Glessner Co, Findlay, OH (from Kiger's Drug Store, Bowling Green, OH), "for children's coughs, colds, chest and throat irritation," ⅜-fl oz, 1½″ × 1″ × 3½″ clear glass bottle in black, red, and white box with black and white letters, child's silhouette, 2 fl oz clear glass bottle, full 8.50

Baby Bottle Warmer, Hankscraft, USA, china nonelectric bottle warmer, "fill to line with hot water, place bottle in warmer for 5 minutes," 3½″ × 3½″ round china vase in 4″ × 4″ × 3½″ dark pink, blue, and white box, picture of a baby hugging stuffed bunny on three sides of box **23.00**

Binky's Bottle Caps, Eagle Druggists Supply Co Inc, New York, USA, "Hand-D-Tab" bottle caps, keeps formula contamination-free, fits narrow-neck bottles, box of two rubber caps in 1⅜″ × 1″ × 2″ pink, blue, and white box with blue and white letters, drawing of two caps on front, full box **6.00**

Capson Baby Bottle Sterilizer, Capson Mfg Co, Chicago, IL, Model "E" aluminum sterilizer rack, pan, funnel, with a nipple jar and cap, six-bottle capacity (nipples and caps in special jar), also sterilizes fruit jars, original 12″ × 9¾″ × 4½″ box with white label and red letters, instruction sheet, **22.00**

Cartose, H. W. Kinney & Sons Inc, Columbus, IN, USA, "mixes carbohydrates for infant feeding," 1-pt round clear glass bottle with yellow, brown, and white label, new label adopted January 1948 **6.50**

Davol Anti-Colic Nipples, Davol Rubber Co, Providence, RI, USA, three anticolic nipples in 2⅛″ × 2⅛″ × 2⅛″ black, light blue, and white box, picture of an anticolic nipple on front, full box **4.00**

Davol Breast Shield, Davol Rubber Co, Providence, RI, No. 807 Amber "Pure Gum" rubber breast shield in 2½″ × 1″ × 2½″ light blue, dark blue, and white box with dark blue and white letters, picture of breast shield on top of box, one breast shield **3.50**

Evenflo Nipple Cover, The Pyramid Rubber Co, Ravenna, OH, USA, "super plastic genuine hospital nipple cover, use on plastic nursers only," box of three covers in 1⅞″ × 3½″ × 1⅞″ pink, tan, light blue, and brown box with brown and white letters, two covers left in box **7.00**

Formi-Keep, Gunn of Grand Rapids, Grand Rapids, MI, "mothers' and infants' fiberglass insulated bag, keeps food or formula hot or cold, best quality washable plastics," beige and wine bag, two zippered side pockets, large zippered inner compartment, double stitched, reinforced shoulder strap, in 13″ × 3⅞″ × 10½″ beige, brown, and tan original box. **18.00**

Kayware Baby Cup, Kayware Corp, Chicago, IL, twin-handled, "molded solidly in

Glass Measuring Pitcher, "Glasco," 1 qt with red letters and numbers, pour lip **12.00**

Heat 'N Serve Baby Dish, General Electric Co, Bridgeport, CT, "heats food, keeps it warm all through feeding," detachable electric cord, three-sectioned dish, picture of a bunny in middle of dish, 12″ × 6″ × 2½″ wine and white box, picture of a baby and many types of baby carriages on top **20.00**

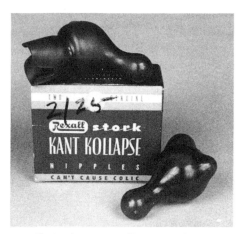

Rexall "Stork" Kant Kollapse Nipples, Rexall Drug Co, Los Angeles, Boston, St. Louis, USA; Toronto, CAN; "the air vent in Stork Kant Kollapse nipple eliminates vacuum, prevents baby from drawing in air, preventing colic," two nipples with comfortable feeding angle, in 2½" × 2" × 1¼" pink, gray, blue, and white box with pink, gray, blue, and white letters, full box **7.50**

one piece from Lustrex, The Royal Plastic," 7-fl oz, cup, "BABY" embossed on front of cup, in 3½" × 2¾" × 3¼" tan, light blue, and dark blue box, picture of cup on front and back of box **10.00**

Nursmatic Conversion Set, Nursmatic Corp, Crystal Lake, IL, three Nursmatic nipples and three Insta-Valves in 3¼" × 1⅞" × 1½" pink, blue, and white box with pink, blue, and white letters, instruction sheet **4.00**

Pyrex Nursing Bottle, Corning Glass Works, Corning, NY, 4-oz narrow-neck embossed clear glass bottle in red, white, and blue cardboard outer "sleeve," silhouette of man blowing glass **10.50**

Stork Sealing Discs, Rexal Drug Co, Los Angeles, Toronto, plastic discs fit stork and most popular nursers, on a 5¾" × ¾" × 1¾" cardholder, three plastic discs sealed in cellophane **7.50**

Tuffy Delux Complete Nursing Unit, Brockway Glass Co Inc, Brockway, PA,

nipple, bottle, and cap with the nipple that "breathes." 8-oz, 6-sided embossed clear glass bottle in pink, navy, and white cardboard outer "sleeve," picture of a baby drinking from bottle, use and care folder **7.00**

INFANT AND CHILDREN LAXATIVES

Fruity-flavored orange-mint De-Witt's Laxative Syrup was a kindly laxative for little bowels; it helped alleviate constipation, improper feedings, and colic. Parents also turned to "Syrup of Black Draught" for their children, a laxative also popular with adults.

Laxatives were never to be used when abdominal pain, nausea, vomiting, or other symptoms of appendicitis were present.

DeWitt's Laxative Syrup, E. C. DeWitt & Co, Inc, Chicago, IL, "orange and mint fruity flavor children's laxative," 3 oz clear glass bottle in 2" × 1¼" × 5⅝" blue, pink, and black box with blue, black, and white letters, picture of mountains, sunset, and three smiling children on front and back of box, advertisement and instruction sheet, almost-full bottle **10.00**

Glycerin Suppositories, Parke, Davis & Co, Detroit, MI, "infant laxative," twelve suppositories, round brown bottle in 1½" × 3½" × 1½" wine and white box with wine and white letters, full bottle **5.00**

Syrup of Black-Draught, The Chattanooga Medicine Co, Chattanooga, TN, "pleasant tasting laxative," 2-fl oz clear glass bottle in 2⅛" × 1⅛" × 5¾" black, yellow, and white box with black and white letters, picture of boy and girl on front, ¾-full bottle **8.75**

Teething Powders, C. J. Moffett Medicine Co, Columbus, GA, "constipation, diarrhea, and colic powder," twelve inch powder box, each individually wrapped in paper, all wrapped together in foil-lined paper in 3¼" × ¼" × 1⅛" black and white box with black letters, picture of a smiling

*Mother Gray's Sweet Powders for Children, Allen S. Olmsted, LeRoy, NY, USA, "laxative powders," 16 powders, in 3″ × 1⅞″ × ⅞″ tan, black, and white box with black letters, picture of "Mother Gray" on top, signature of Allen S. Olmsted on one end of box, full unopened box **7.50***

*Mexsana Baby Oil, Plough Inc, New York, NY; Memphis, TN; San Francisco, CA; "soothes and protects baby's tender skin," 4-fl oz clear glass bottle with 2½″ × 1″ × 6″ pink and white label with blue letters, picture of happy baby on front, full bottle **8.75***

baby, Charles J. Moffett's signature, 24 postage postcards, instruction sheet, full box **8.00**

INFANT AND CHILDREN SKIN PRODUCTS

Johnson's baby oil was a trusted product to apply to baby's tender skin. Some products contained lanolin. Tender Age Calamine Lotion provided relief from the discomfort of prickly heat, diaper rash, chafing, hives, and other minor skin irritations.

Baby Ointment, The S. E. Massengill Co, Bristol, TN, "soothing antiseptic ointment," 1-oz tube in 1¼″ × ¼″ × 4⅝″ blue, pink, white, yellow, and brown box with blue, pink, white, yellow, and brown letters, "baby" spelled out in blocks, one on top of the other, almost-full tube **4.75**

Desitin Baby Lotion, Desitin Chemical Co, Providence, RI, "antiseptic, cleansing, soothing lotion," 4-fl oz clear glass bottle in 2½″ × 1½″ × 5½″ blue and white box with blue, white, and red letters, picture of a baby, almost-full bottle **7.50**

"Pedameth," S. F. Durst & Co Inc, Ol-Methionine, "oral treatment of diaper rash," 30 caps, round brown bottle in 1½″ × 2¾″ × 1½″ pink and navy box with white and navy letters, instruction sheet, full unopened bottle **5.00**

Tender Age Calamine Lotion, Nyal Co, Detroit, MI, "soothing and healing lotion," 6-fl oz clear glass bottle, 2½″ × 1″ × 6½″ pink, blue, and white label with blue and white letters, picture of three babies on front, almost-empty bottle **10.00**

INFANT AND CHILDREN VITAMINS

Taste was essential in making vitamins palatable to children. Some vitamins had a delicious fruity flavor and simply dissolved in the mouth, which made taking the vitamins more fun. In many cases, the vitamins retain their pungent odor even after having been removed from the drugstore shelves for years.

St. Joseph Vitamins for Children, Plough Inc,
Los Angeles, New York, Memphis, Miami,
"chewable multiple vitamins for the whole
family, five delicious flavors," 60 tabs, clear
glass bottle in 3⅝" × 1¾" × 1⅝" blue,
pink, and white box with black, pink, and
white letters, picture of boy and girl on front,
picture of fruit on sides, instruction sheet,
full bottle **3.00**

Children's Vitamin Capsules, Kiger's Drug
Store, Bowling Green, OH, 100 caps, 3¾"
× 2⅜" round green bottle with black
metal cap, pink, blue, and white label with
blue and white letters, picture of young
boy and girl, full bottle **7.00**

Squibb Viosterol in Oil, E. R. Squibb & Sons,
New York, contains 10,000 U.S.P. × 1 vitamin D units per gram, 5-cc octagonal blue
bottle with gold metal cap, dropper and
cap in 1¾" × 1¼" × 2¾" yellow and
brown box with brown letters, full bottle
7.00

LAYETTE ITEMS

Mennen's baby oil, Johnson's Baby
Soap, and Diaperene Baby Lotion were
utilitarian items in a baby's nursery.

Little Lady "Her Very Own Toiletries" Hand Lotion was an early product designed especially for little girls.
The Brother & Sister Bath Set contained
both hand soap and bubble bath. One
bar of soap and one bottle of bubble
bath featured a picture of a little boy
while the other set had a picture of a
little girl.

An unusual complimentary gift
package was presented to every family
with a new baby by Woodruff's Pharmacy in Owensville, Ohio. The package
contained an assortment of sample
items, including Chocks Multiple Vitamins, Vaseline White Petroleum Jelly,
Nupercainal Anesthetic Ointment,
Gelusil (for heartburn), Massengill
Douche Powder, and Coetes Quilted
Squares. A postcard from the Mutual
Benefit Life Insurance Company was included. By mailing the postcard, a complimentary copy of Dr. Spock's *Baby
and Child Care* was "yours for the ask-
ing."

Ammorid Diaper Rinse, Kinney & Co Inc,
Columbus, IN, "acts directly on the orga-
nisms responsible for ammonia formation,
helps prevent diaper rash, powder," 240-
gram (8.46 oz), 4¾" × 2½" round brown
bottle, yellow and white label with brown
letters, full bottle **7.00**

Baby's Comb, France, "fine tooth combs for
baby and children," ten 4⅝" × ¾" tan,
olive, and pink combs on 10" × 12" light
and dark blue display card that can be
hung up, picture of mother, baby, and girl
in bathroom in dark blue, "Baby" and
"France" written in gold on combs, ten
combs **40.00**

Binky's Soother, Binky Baby Products Co,
New York City, NY, "odorless and tasteless
teether, non-porous, stays fresh, safe for
the tiniest infant, practically indestructible,
withstands repeated sterilizing," one in
pink, light blue, white, dark blue, red, and
tan in 3½" × 4" clear plastic and cardboard

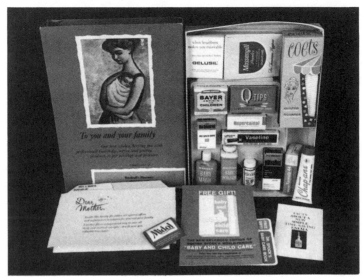

Complimentary Gift Set, Woodruff's Pharmacy, Owensville, OH, "for new mothers and family," 14" × 9¾" × 2¾" blue, white, orange gift box with black lettering, picture of mother and baby, includes all of the following items:

Baby Magic, The Mennen Co, Morristown, NJ; Toronto, ONT, "baby lotion," 1¼-fl oz, 1¾" × 1" × 3¼" blue plastic bottle with white letters, professional size.

Baby Powder, The Mennen Co., Morristown, NJ; Toronto, ONT, 1½-oz, 1⅜" × 1⅜" × 4" blue and white baby powder tin with shaker top with white letters.

Bayer Aspirin for Children, The Bayer Co, Div of Sterling Drug Co, New York, NY, two tabs, in paper packets in 2½" × 2" × ¾" in blue, pink, white, and red box with blue and red letters. Six paper packets.

Chap-ans, Chap Stick Co, Div Morton Mfg Co, Lynchburg, VA, "medicated hand lotion," 1.25-ox, ¾" × 4½" white plastic tube, red cap with red and black letters.

Chocks, Miles Products, Elkhart, IN, "chewable multiple vitamins, fruit flavored," ten tabs, 1" × 2¼" clear glass bottle, green and white label with red and green letters.

Coets, Personal Products Co, Milltown, NJ, 40 quilted cosmetic squares in 6¼" × 2⅝" × 2" pink, blue, white, and light blue box with blue letters, picture of woman.

Formula 44, Vicks Chemical Co, Div of Richardson-Merrell Inc, New York, NY, ½-oz, 3" × 2" × 1" sealed brown glass bottle in green, white, and blue box with green and blue letters, free sample, trial size.

Massengill, The S. E. Massengill Co, Briston, TN, "douche powder," two foil packets in 4½" × 3⅛" yellow, red, and white paper pouch with red and white letters.

Midol, Glenbrook Labs, Div of Sterling Drug, Inc, New York, NY, "fast relief of functional menstrual pain," five tabs, 2" × 2⅜" blue and white matchbook type package with white and dark blue letters.

Neo-Synephrine, Winthrop Labs, Div of Sterling Drug Inc, New York, NY, "nasal spray for children," 3-ml plastic squeeze bottle in 1½" × 2¼" × ¾" pink and white box with pink and blue letters.

Nupercainal, Ciba Pharmaceutical, Summit, NJ, "anesthetic ointment," 5-gm aluminum tube in ¾" × 1" × 3" red, white, and blue box with red and blue letters, sample not to be sold.

Paper file folder containing fleet enema information pamphlet, free gift card for Dr. Spock's baby care book, 9" × 7".

Phisohex, Winthrop Labs, New York, NY, "sudsing antibacterial skin cleaner," 1-fl oz round plastic squeeze bottle in 1½" × 1½" × 3¼" green, white, and black box with black and white letters.

Q-Tips, The Chesebrough-Pond's Inc, New York, NY, "sterilized cotton swabs" commended by Parents Magazine and Guaranteed by Good Housekeeping," box of ten swabs in 3⅜" × 2" × ⅜" blue, white, and dark blue box with dark blue and white letters, cellophane-wrapped box.

Vaseline, Chesbrough-Pond's, New York, NY, "white petroleum jelly," The First Aid Kit in a Tube, large-size 3.5-oz aluminum tube with plastic cap in 1" × 1" × 4¼" blue and white box with blue and white letters.

Complete unopened Gift Set—*42.00*

package with dark blue, white, and black letters, picture of a baby and toys, **7.00**

Binky's Thum Gard, Binky Baby Products Co, New York City, USA, "aids in preventing thumb and finger sucking," adjustable, stainless-steel slotted thumb guard with ribbon to tie around wrist to keep guard on thumb, in 1″ × 1″ × 1¾″ navy, pink, and white box with navy and white letters, picture of hand with guard on **8.50**

Cradle Joy, Murray Toy & Novelty Co, Hagerstown, MD, "baby's perfect crib toy," wooden block and other shaped toys on rope to hang over crib, all in 4¼″ × 12½″ × 1″ tan box with pink and black label and black letters, wooden toys are light blue, red, tan, and yellow, Pat. Nov. 24, 1942 **20.00**

Curity Diaper Liners, Kendall Mills, Div of the Kendall Co, Walpole, MA, disposable paper diaper liners, 152 boxed in 6″ × 1″

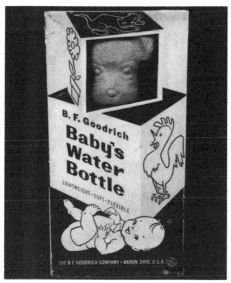

Baby's Water Bottle, The B. F. Goodrich Co, Akron, OH, USA, "rubber water bottle to keep baby warm or cool," one pink puppy water bottle, one-piece construction, leakproof, rustproof stopper in 5¼″ × 1½″ × 10¼″ green, yellow, and white plastic-wrapped box with green and white letters, picture of happy baby with water bottle on tummy **30.00**

× 14″ navy, pink, and white box with navy, pink, and white letters, bottom of box advertises other Curity products with words and pictures, diapers, nursery pads, bibs, etc., Copyright 1954 **12.00**

Johnson's Baby Cream, Johnson & Johnson, New Brunswick, NJ, "allergy safe, protects and heals tender baby skin," 1 oz milk glass jar with pink metal cap, pink and white label with blue and white letters, full jar **5.00**

Johnson's Baby Soap, Johnson & Johnson, New Brunswick, NJ, "pure bland castile soap for gentle cleansing," one bar in plain white paper wrapper in 2″ × 3¼″ × 1″ pink and white box with navy and white letters **6.00**

Koroseal Baby Pants, The B. F. Goodrich Co, Akron, OH, snap-on baby pants, one pair in 3¾″ × ⅞″ × 7″ pink, light blue, and white box with dark brown and light blue letters, picture of happy baby on top **10.00**

Little Lady Hand Lotion, Helene Pessl, Inc, New York, NY, "her very own toiletries," 4-fl oz, 6″ × 1½″ round clear glass bottle, pink and tan hard plastic pump cap, pink, light and dark blue, brown, and white label with black letters, ⅔-full bottle **13.00**

Lor-Bet Bonnet, Lor-Bet Mfg Co, Chicago, IL, "adjustable baby bonnet, grows with the baby," drawstring allows bonnet to be adjusted for a 5-day-old to 18 months, light blue and white nylon bonnet and tie straps, white lace trim around face, drawstring in back to adjust size, 6″ × 10″ × 1″ light blue and white box with white letters, bonnet viewed through plastic-covered oval opening in lid of box, instruction sheet **32.00**

Mennen Baby Oil, The Mennen Co, Morristown, NJ; Toronto, ONT, cleansing oil with mineral oil and lanolin, 12-oz clear glass bottle, pale blue, red, and dark blue label and letters, embossed rose, "Mennen" and "grip" lines, full bottle **11.00**

Playtex Baby Powder, Drug Div, International Latex Corp, Playtex Park, Dover, DE, "antiseptic powder, expressly for babies, soothes newborn skin from head to toe,"

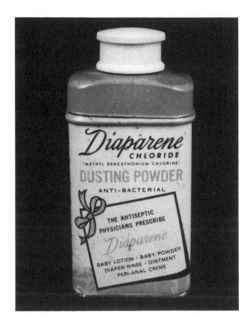

Diaparene Chloride Dusting Powder, Home-makers Products Corp, New York, NY; Toronto, CAN, "anti-bacterial, no boric acid powder," ¾-oz, 1¼" × 1" × 2¾" white, black, and light blue tin with black and light blue letters, almost-full tin **15.00**

6-oz, 5¼" × 2¼" gold, white, and blue cardboard cylinder, metal bottom, plastic shaker top, pink and blue letters, almost-full cylinder, dated 1948 **10.00**

Playtex Bib-Smock, International Latex Corp, super size for 2–6 years, plastic bib-smock, white bib-smock with multi-colored dots in light blue and pink clear plastic and cardboard package with black and light blue letters, dated 1956 **10.00**

Rubber Deflector, Sanitoy, USA, "for all nursery seats and training chairs," light blue soft sanitary rubber deflector in 4¾" × 1¾" × 3¾" pink, blue, and white box with pink, blue, and white letters **5.75**

Twin-Turtle, "baby's bib holder," light blue plastic turtles, adjustable tape straps, "makes any towel or napkin a perfect bib," encased in clear, round, hard plastic 3¼" × ⅞" advertisement cardboard, white, red, and light blue cardboard box with red and dark blue letters, circle has drawing of

baby's head on front, picture of baby in high chair on back **8.00**

TEETHING PRODUCTS

Thum, Num Specialty Co Inc, "discourages thumb sucking and nail biting," 2-dram clear glass bottle with plastic applicator cap, blue and white label and letters, almost-full bottle **5.00**

Tots Teething Cream, Kraupner Pharmaceutical Co, Brooklyn, NY, "relieves teething pains and toothache," ⅓-oz tube of cream in 3⅞" × ⅞" × ⅝" pale blue and white box with black and pale blue letters, picture of happy baby on top and bottom of box, almost-full tube **5.25**

Gold Medal Gum Lotion, S. Pfeiffer Mfg Co, St. Louis, MO, "infants sore gum and toothache lotion," 3-fl oz, 2⅛" × 1⅜" × 6" clear glass bottle in red, gold, and white box with black, gold, and white letters, instruction sheet, ½-full bottle **8.00**

MISCELLANEOUS INFANT AND CHILDREN MEDICINAL PRODUCTS

When collecting items in this category, look for unusual products such as the Davol Rubber Company's Infant Specimen Collectors.

Babee Nose Drops, The Pfeiffer Co, St. Louis, MO, "relieves nasal congestion in colds, hay fever," ½-fl oz clear glass bottle, dropper in unopened cellophane wrap, 2" × 1⅜" × 3⅜" pink, white, and blue box with pink, blue, and white letters, picture of a baby head and medicine dropper, ¾-full bottle **4.00**

Children's Aspirin, The Norwich Pharmacal Co, Norwich, NY, "relieves simple headaches, discomforts of colds, muscle aches and pains," 50 sweet orange-flavored tablets in clear glass bottle, 1½" × 1" × 2⅞" blue and white box with black and white letters, no top, full bottle **6.50**

Children's Soltice, The Chattanooga Medicine Co, Chattanooga, TN, "mild quickrub, relieves colds and minor sore muscle distresses," round blue jar in 1⅞" × 1⅞" × 2½" pink, navy, and white box with navy letters, picture of heads of happy boy

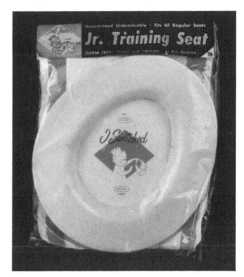

*Junior Training Seat, Earl Fisher Plastic Co, Columbus, OH, baby toilet-training seat, "Hi-impact plastic, guaranteed unbreakable, fits all regular seats, germ free, treated with corobex, an antibacterial," one pink plastic training seat in 12" × 15" sealed clear plastic bag with pink, white, navy, red, and yellow cardboard tops with red, yellow, and white letters, cardboard has picture of a baby wearing a gold crown, winking, holding a diaper saying, "I switched," and picture of a toilet seat with baby training seat on it **12.00***

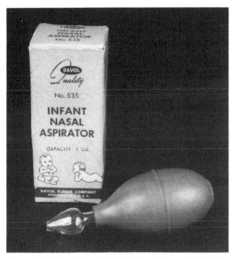

*Davol Infant Nasal Aspirator, Davol Rubber Co, Providence, RI, USA, "for extracting mucofluids from the nasal cavities," rubber bulb and glass-tip aspirator in 1¾" × 1¾" × 4" light blue, dark blue, and tan box with dark blue and white letters, pictures of four babies and the aspirator on front and sides of box, instruction sheet **6.50***

and girl on box top, instructions and advertisement sheet, almost-full jar **7.00**

Davol Infant Specimen Collectors, Davol Rubber Co, Providence, RI, USA, "urine sample collection bags," 12 individual plastic-wrapped bags, adhesive surface to attach to infant, adhesive seals bag when specimen obtained, 4" × 3¼" × 1" tan box with blue letters, full box of 12 **24.00 or 2.00 each**

Pediatric Neo-Synephrine, Winthrop Labs, Div of Sterling Drug Inc, New York, NY, "nasal spray for congestion in head colds and hay fever," 20-cc white plastic squeeze bottle with pink cap in 2½" × 1⅜" × 2⅞" blue, pink, and white box with blue and white letters, ¾-full bottle **8.00**

Kidney/Urinary Products

Sluggish kidneys can result in painful backache, nagging headaches and dizziness, rheumatic pains, swelling and puffiness, frequent or difficult urination, and lack of pep and energy. Herb tablets and many forms of diuretics were intended to alleviate all of these symptoms and ills.

Arbutin, Swan Myers Co, Pharmaceutical & Biological Laboratories, Indianapolis, IN, "stimulating diuretic, for diseases of the genito-urinary tract," 100 tabs, small brown cork-stopper bottle with black and white label **7.50**

Citrasulfas, The Upjohn Co, Kalamazoo, MI, "to be dispensed only by or on the prescription of physician, may cause toxic re-

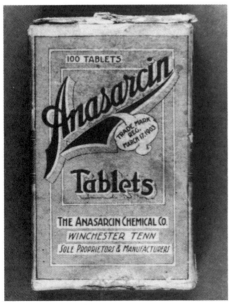

Anasarcin Tablets, The Anasarcin Chemical Co, Winchester, TN, diuretic and laxative, 100 tabs, 2¼" × 1⅜" × 1" orange and black tin container with black letters in 2¼" × 1½" × 1" orange and black cardboard box with black letters, instruction sheet, trademark registered March 17, 1903, full tin in unopened box **40.00**

actions," 1-pt round brown bottle, gold and white label with black letters **8.50**

Cystogen-Lithia, Cystogen Chemical Co, Jersey City, NJ, "effervescent tablets, treatment of genitary urinary tract," 12 tabs, glass cork-stoppered vials, in 3¼" × 2" × ¾" orange box with white label and orange and black letters, instruction folder, 3 vials **14.00**

Dr. J. H. McLean's Universal Pills, The Dr. J. H. McLean Med Co, St. Louis, MO, USA, "liver complaints," cork-stoppered brown bottle in 2½" × 1¼" × 1" black and white box with black and white letters, doctor's name embossed on side of bottle, Dr. J. H. McLean signature on box to prevent counterfeiting, dated 1919, instruction folder, full bottle **15.00**

Dr. Pierce's "A-Nuric" tablets, Pierce's Proprietaries Inc, New York, NY, "diuretic to the kidneys and analgesic for muscular aches and pains," 100 tabs, round clear glass bottle with black metal cap in 3½" × 1¾" × 1¾" blue and white box with black and white letters, instruction folder, full bottle **7.00**

Foley Pills, Foley & Co, Chicago, IL, "a diuretic stimulant for kidneys," 40 pills, brown bottle with brown and gold metal cap in 3" × 1½" × 1⅛" orange, black, and tan box with black and tan letters, instruction folder, full bottle **3.25**

Furadantin Brand of Nitrofurantion, Eston Laboratories, Div of the Norwich Pharmacal Co, Norwich, NY, "urinary tract antibacterial," 60 cc of gel, brown bottle with metal cap, in 3½" × 2" × 1½" pale green, white, and black box with black and white letters, instruction folder, ½-full bottle **4.75**

Gold Medal "B & J Pills," S. Pfeiffer Mfg Co, St. Louis, MO, "diuretic stimulant to the kidneys," 20 pills, round glass cork-stoppered vial in red, gold, and tan box with black and tan letters, full vial **10.00**

Martin's Herb Tablets, The Martin Herb Co, no address, "kidney and liver regulator, blood purifier," 3" × 1½" × ½" white, green, and orange box with white and orange letters, empty box **6.00**

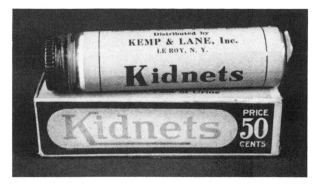

*Kidnets, Kemp & Lane Inc, Le-Roy, NY, "kidney stimulant," 45 pills, round glass vial with blue metal cap in 3½" × 1" × 1" two-tone green and tan box with black, red, and white letters, full vial **5.00***

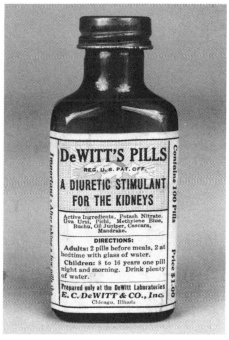

*DeWitt's Pills, E. C. DeWitt Co Inc, Chicago, IL, "diuretic stimulant for kidneys," 100 pills, 3½" × 1½" × 1" brown bottle with wine-colored metal cap, red and white label with black letters, picture of mountaintop, ½ full bottle **3.50***

Rival Herb Tablets, The Rival Herb Co, Detroit, MI; Montreal, CAN, "digestion, liver, kidney, blood, etc., a true family medicine," 3¼" × 2¼" × 1½" red, gold, and black tin with red, gold, and black letters, empty tin **12.00**

Sonilyn (Sulfachlor-Pyridazine), Mallinckrodt Chemical Works, St. Louis, MO, "urinary infections," 100 tabs, brown glass bottle in 3¾" × 2" × 1⅜" orange, tan, pale gray box with black, white, and orange letters, ¾-full bottle **5.00**

Urothropin, Schering & Glatz, Inc, New York, St. Louis, "urinary antiseptic," 30 tabs, individual "cells" in strips of cellophane in 2½" × 1¾" × ⅞" yellow and white box with red and black letters, six tabs left **8.00**

Warner's Compound, Warner's Remedies Co Inc, Rochester, NY, "kidney stimulant," 40 tabs, brown bottle with black plastic cap in 3" × 1½" × 1" dark blue and tan box with dark blue letters, instruction folder, full bottle **5.00**

Laxatives

Not only were there laxatives, cathartics, purgatives, and laxative cold tablets in the old-time pharmacy, but laxative tonics, laxative liver regulators, teas, herbs, and suppositories also helped contribute to the most popular aisle in the old drugstore. Stockboys and clerks were kept busy replenishing shelves of liquids, syrups, tablets, and an assortment of miscellaneous products.

Biliousness, torpid liver, malarial conditions, heartburn, flatulence, dizziness, and some forms of headaches could be attributed to constipation. Any medication designed to move the bowels was *not* to be used when abdominal pain, nausea, vomiting, or other signs of appendicitis were present. Most of the packages cautioned that allergic individuals should discontinue use if a rash appeared and that habitual use could result in a dependence on laxatives.

LAXATIVE LIQUIDS

Dr. Thacher's Laxative Compound contained senna and rhubarb and supposedly was gentle and effective. Since the laxative was liquid, exact dosages were easily regulated. The alcohol content was six percent. Norolar Plain, however, contained no alcohol, alkalies, or sugar. Diabetics who suffered from constipation could use this laxative without upsetting their carbohydrate balance.

The French Lick Springs Hotel Company of French Lick, Indiana, distributed Pluto, which was "America's Physic." Sodium sulphate and magnesium sulphate were the principal ingredients in the concentrated and fortified spring water. Successful results were achieved when the liquid was diluted with hot water.

Adlerika, Adlerika Co, Baltimore, MD, USA, "temporary relief of occasional constipation," 12-fl oz, 6½" × 2½" × 1¾" brown glass bottle with white metal lid, yellow and black label with red and black letters **5.75**

Cascara-Lax, distr by Modern Drugs Inc, Philippi WV, "a pleasant, mild, and effective laxative," 2-fl oz, 3¾" × 1⅝" × 1" brown glass bottle with black plastic lid, blue, red, and white label with blue and white letters, full bottle **2.75**

Dr. Thacher's Laxative Compound of Senna and Rhubarb, Thacher Medicine Co, Chattanooga, TN, 2-fl oz, 3¾" × 1¼" brown glass bottle with white metal lid in 4¼" ×

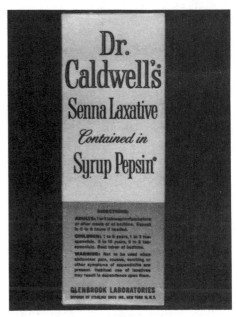

Dr. Caldwell's Senna Laxative, Glenbrook Laboratories, Div of Sterling Drug Inc, New York, NY, "a gentle effective laxative for the whole family," 5-fl oz, 6½" × 2¼" × 1" clear glass bottle with orange metal lid in 7" × 2½" × 1¼" orange and yellow cardboard box, picture of a family, full bottle **8.50**

1½" × 1½" orange cardboard box with black letters, full jar **8.00**

Doxinate 5%, Lloyd Brothers, Cincinnati, OH, USA, "an aid in the treatment of temporary constipation," 2-fl oz, 3½" × 2" × 1⅜" brown glass bottle with black plastic lid in 4" × 3" × 1½" gray and white box with black letters, dropper included, almost-full bottle **8.00**

Forni's Alpen Krauter Laxative, Dr. Peter Fahrney & Sons Co mfr and sole proprietors, Chicago, IL, USA; Winnipeg, Manitoba, Canada, "for relief from constipation and the following symptoms: upset stomach, indigestion, coated tongue, flatulence, loss of appetite, headache, nervousness, restlessness, and loss of sleep," 18-fl oz, 9" × 7½" × 2½" clear glass bottle with green metal lid, white label with green

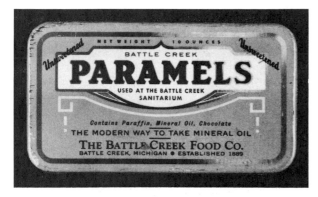

Paramels, The Battle Creek Food Co, Battle Creek, MI, established 1889, "mineral oil in pleasant tasting caramel form," 10-oz, 1⅝" × 6" × 3½" orange, gold, black, and white metal box with black and gold letters, "used at the Battle Creek Sanitarium," empty box **75.00**

Pluto Spring Water, Pluto Corp, French Lick, IN, laxative, "America's Laxative," 2¼-fl oz, 4½" × 1½" round green bottle, with red and black letters on red, white, green, and yellow label, red Pluto (devil) on label face and bottle cap, Pluto embossed on bottle bottom, drawing of company building on label, ¾-full bottle **42.00**
8 fl oz, full bottle **50.00**

letters, "none genuine without this signature: P. Fahrney, M.D.," full bottle **15.00**

Maltine, The Maltine Co, New York, Est. 1875, "a valuable aid in the treatment of constipation and intestinal indigestion arising from defective bile action," 8-fl oz, 5½" × 2¾" × 2" brown glass jar with gold metal lid in 5¾" × 3" × 2¼" brown cardboard box with black and red letters, full jar **13.00**

Norolar, The Norwich Pharmacal Co, Norwich, NY, makers of Unguentine and Pepto-Bismol, "for constipation and bowel sluggishness," 1-pt, 8" × 2¾" clear glass bottle with yellow, red, and black label with yellow and black letters, full bottle **12.00**

Prune Malt, Benson-Nuen Laboratories Inc, distr, subsidiary of Homemakers Products Corp, New York, NY; Toronto, CAN, "dietary aid to bowel regulation in infants, children, and adults," 8-fl oz, 4¾" × 2¼" brown glass jar with black metal lid, gold and tan label with black and red letters, pictures of prunes and leaves, full jar **15.00**

LAXATIVE POWDERS

Sal Hepatica, produced by Bristol-Myers, and Saraka, manufactured by the Schering Corporation, appeared in various types of packaging. Sal Hepatica was first distributed in small vials in an attractive dark blue and white box with flowers on top. A small trial-size tin of Saraka reminded the customer, "Do not chew the granules." (**Collecting Hint:** This is one of the tins that is highly desirable because of color, name brand, size, and composition of tin.)

The Battle Creek Food Company of Battle Creek, Michigan, introduced Lacto Dextrin, "a food for changing the intestinal flora." This formula was first prepared and tested at the Battle Creek Sanitarium. Best test results were achieved when the powder was mixed in a large tumbler of water and stirred until smooth, then mixed with more water, preferably hot. The best results were achieved when used with mineral oil, bran, or agar. This medication was to be taken upon arising in the morning and three to four hours after every meal.

Myers Laboratories, Inc., of Warren, Pennsylvania, manufactured "Thialion," which was a noneffervescing lithiated salt.

Psyllium Seed, packaged by Purepac Corp, New York, NY; Chicago, IL; Los Angeles, CA, laxative, 1-lb, 5" × 3¾" × 2½" pink and maroon metal box with green letters, full box **8.00**

Cellothyl, Chilcott Laboratories, Inc, formerly The Maltine Co, Morris Plains, NJ, est. 1875, "corrective treatment of constipation," 25-gram, 3¼" × 1½" × 1½" brown glass bottle with black metal lid, white and blue label with black letters, almost-full bottle **5.00**

Lacto-Dextrin, The Battle Creek Food Co, Battle Creek, MI, USA, "a food for changing the intestinal flora," 12-oz, 5" × 3" gold metal can, orange label with red and black letters, full can **25.00**

Rochelle Salt, USP, distr by Blake Pharmacal Co, Allegan, MI, "laxative," 2-oz, 1⅞" × 2" metal can, black and orange label with black letters, full can **4.00**

Sal Hepatica, Compliments of Bristol-Myers Co, New York, "laxative powder," clear glass vials with aluminum caps, in 4¾" × 7" × 2⅝" dark blue and white box with lift-off top, dark blue and yellow letters, two yellow flowers on box top, five empty vials **20.00**

Ru-Co Collins Laboratories, Memphis, TN, "a simple saline laxative, produces copious discharges from the bowl," 8½-oz, 5⅜" × 2" × 2" clear glass bottle with metal lid, green and gray label with white and black letters, full bottle **8.00**

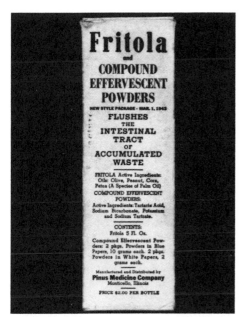

Fritola and Compound Effervescent Powders, mfr and distr by Pinüs Medicine Co, Monticello, Il., "flushes the intestinal tract of accumulated waste," 5-fl oz, 6½″ × 2″ × 1¼″ clear glass bottle with cork stopper top, 24-gram, 7″ × 2″ cellophane envelope in 6¾″ × 2″ × 2⅛″ brown cardboard box with black letters, new-style package, Mar. 1, 1943, instruction sheet, business reply card, full bottle and envelope **10.00**

Saraka, made in USA by Schering Corp, Bloomfield, NJ, "for constipation," ¾ oz, 2¼″ × 1″ × 1½″ orange and yellow metal container with black letters, empty container **35.00**

Testarr, Testagar & Co, Inc, distr Detroit, MI, "useful in the treatment of most common types of constipation and such forms of bowel dysfunction as the physician may consider it indicated," 5¼″ × 4½″ × 3⅛″ metal container, blue and white label with blue and white letters, full container **9.00**

LAXATIVE TABLETS

Nature's Remedy, Cascarets, and Ex-Lax were popular laxative tablets. One old advertising mirror distributed by Cascarets featured a small child sitting on a china pot with the message "Everything going out, nothing coming in." A product called "Clock-Lax" prominently displayed a clock on the front of the tin that noted "Acts On Time."

Lydia E. Pinkham's Pills For Constipation acted in harmony with Lydia E. Pinkham's Vegetable Compound. Both were purely vegetable laxatives. Burtone's Lower Bowel and General Laxative "Acts when you need it." Dare's motto for its Pink Purgative Pills was "The little pink pill that says I will." Dr. Pierce manufactured Pleasant Pellets, while the Iron-Ox Remedy Company of Detroit considered its Laxative Iron-Ox Tablets as strong as an ox.

Once Ex-Lax distributed its product, a "Lax" competition began. Smile-Lax, Charm-Lax, Tasty-Lax (both sample and regular), Dime-Lax, and Lax-A-Mint engulfed the market.

Allenru Laxative Pills, mfr especially for Alle-Rhume Co, Jersey City, NJ, "laxative pills," 36 pills, 3″ × 1″ wooden cylinder in 3″ × 1⅛″ × 1⅛″ red and white cardboard box with red and white letters, full unopened cylinder **7.50**

Argotane, Argotane Co, Div of Plough Inc, New York, Memphis, "intestinal tonic, laxative, chola-gogue, appetizer," ¼″ × 1¼″ × 1¾″ green and yellow metal box with green and yellow letters, full cellophane-sealed physician's sample box **4.25**

B.O.L. Tablets, distr by a specialty products div, American Druggists Syndicated Inc, New York, NY, "a laxative for occasional constipation with added vitamin B," 30 tabs, 2½″ × ¾″ × 1¼″ clear glass bottle with white metal lid in 2¾″ × 1⅝″ × ⅞″ red, white, and blue cardboard box with red, white and blue letters, full bottle **7.50**

Black-Draught Tablets, The Chattanooga Medicine Co, Chattanooga, TN, "a pleasant laxative," 30 tabs, 1½″ × 1½″ × 2″ yellow and black cardboard box with black and

Bliss Native Herbs, Alonzo O. Bliss Medical Co, Washington, DC; Montreal, CAN, "the active ingredients of Bliss Native Herbs consist only of nature's own plant materials, they are entirely botanical, these tablets are purposely uncoated so as to make more readily available the stomachic action of the 'bitters,' " 65 tabs, ¾" × 1¾" × 3" yellow cardboard box with red and black letters, instruction sheet, picture of Alonzo O. Bliss, full box **12.00**

Crack Shot Pills, Gattis Chemical Co, Nashville, TN, "for temporary constipation, sour stomach, and billiousness [sic] *due to constipation," 30 pills, 2¼" × ½" clear glass bottle with cork stopper top in ¾" × 2½" × 1" red cardboard box with black letters, picture of man, instruction sheet, full bottle* **8.00**

yellow letters, full cellophane-sealed box **3.50**

Blackstone Tasty-Lax, Blackstone Products Co Inc, New York, NY, "chocolate flavored laxative," ⅜" × 1⅝" × 1⅝" red and gold metal box with red letters, free sample **7.00**

Blakes Herbs Tablets, International Drug Co, Boston, MA, USA, "a mild effective laxative, kidney and liver regulator," 40 tabs, ½" × 1¾" × 2¾" white cardboard box with red and blue letters **6.00**

Booth's Pills, Booth's Hyomel Co, Ithaca, NY; Toronto, ONT, "for constipation, and sick headache, biliousness, torpid liver, melancholy, vertigo, when caused by constipation," 50 pills, 2⅜" × ¾" wooden jar with wooden lid in 3" × 1⅛" cardboard cylinder, white label with red and blue letters, instruction sheet **8.00**

Cascara Cathartic, assayed and distr by McKesson Laboratories, Bridgeport, CT, 100

tabs, 3" × 2" × 1" clear glass bottle with white metal lid, white and yellow label with black letters, full bottle **5.75**

Cascarets Laxative Tablets, Cascarets Inc, distr, Hewlett, NY, "to relieve constipation," 50 tabs, ½" × 3¾" × 2½" blue cardboard box with blue and white letters **4.25**

Chamberlain's tablets, Chamberlain Medicine Co Inc, New York, NY; St. Louis, MO; "for constipation and headache due to constipation," 40 tabs, 2⅜" × 1" × ½" clear glass bottle with black plastic lid in 2½" × 1⅝" × ¾" yellow and white cardboard box with black letters, full bottle **8.00**

Dare's Pink Purgative Pills, prepared for Dare's Mentha Pepsin Co, Bridgeton, NJ, USA, "for constipation, biliousness, lazy liver, sallow skin, headache, bad taste, and foul breath," 30 pills, 2¼" × ¾" × ¾" clear glass bottle with cork stopper in 2¾" × ¾" × ¾" orange cardboard box with

DeWitt's Little Early Risers, Mfr by E. C. DeWitt & Co, Chicago, IL, "laxative and cathartic pills," 27 pills, 2⅝" × ½" green paper-wrapped roll with green letters, picture of sunrise over mountains, full roll **5.00**

Konjola Laxative Tablets, mfr by Mosby Medicine Co, Cincinnati, OH, "highly recommended for use with the Konjola Medicine, especially when constipation is present," 20 tabs, ¾" × ¾" × 3" green and black cardboard box with black letters, full box **7.00**

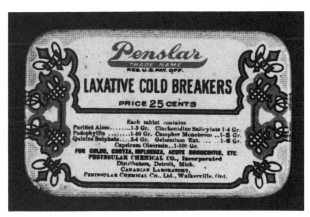

Laxative Cold Breakers, Peninsular Chemical Co, Inc, distr Detroit, MI; Canadian Laboratory, Peninsular Chemical Co LTD, Walkersville, ONT, "for colds, coryza, influenza, acute bronchitis, etc." ½" × 2½" × 1½" gray and white metal container with black letters, full container **8.00**

black and red letters, instruction sheet, full bottle **6.00**

Dr. King's Pills, H. E. Bucklen & Co, offices, New York, St. Louis (formerly Chicago), "for biliousness and constipation," 36 pills, 2¾" × ¾" × ¾" clear glass cork-stoppered bottle in 3" × 1⅛" × 1⅛" brown cardboard box with black letters, full bottle **11.00**

Ex-Lax, prepared only by The Ex-Lax Inc, Brooklyn, NY, "for relief of constipation," 16 tabs, 1" × 2¼" × 3¾" blue and white metal box with blue and red letters, full box **22.00**

Hinkle's Pill N.F., Rexall Drug Co, Los Angeles, Boston, St. Louis, USA; Toronto, CAN, "a valuable laxative for difficult cases of constipation which require a thorough

cleansing cathartic," 500 tabs, 2¾" × 1¼" × ¾" brown glass bottle with white metal lid in 2⅞" × 1½" × 1" yellow and brown cardboard box with yellow and brown letters, full bottle **7.00**

Iron-Ox Tablets, mfr for The Iron-Ox Remedy Co, Detroit, MI, USA; London, ENG; Walkerville, Ont, CAN, "an ideal laxative," 1¾" × ½" × 1" gray and white cardboard box with black letters, full unopened box **8.00**

Lane's Pills, Chas. E. Lane & Co, sole owners and distr, St. Louis, MO, "for occasional constipation use Lane's pills," 20 pills, 2½" × ⅜" clear glass cork-stoppered bottle in 2⅞" × ¾" × ¾" red and white cardboard box with white letters, instruction sheet, full bottle **8.50**

Dr. J. H. McLean's Universal Pills, mfr for The Dr. J. H. Mc-Lean Medical Co, St. Louis, MO, USA, "for liver complaints, biliousness," 2¼" × 1" × ⅝" brown glass bottle with cork stopper top, in 2½" × 1" × 1¼" blue and white cardboard box with blue and white letters, instruction sheet, Spanish translation, full bottle 15.00

NR Jrs, mfr by Lewis-Howe Co, St. Louis, MO, USA, "for conditions caused by or associated with constipation," 36 tabs, ½" × 1½" × 1¼" blue and yellow metal box with blue letters 8.50

Fruitative, Fruitatives Limited, Ogdensburg, NY, "efficient in biliousness, relieves constipation, aids in clearing the complexion, and refreshens the whole system," 36 tabs, 2¾" × 1½" × 1½" pink, blue, and white cardboard box with black letters, pictures of different fruits. "By their fruits ye shall know them," empty box 15.00

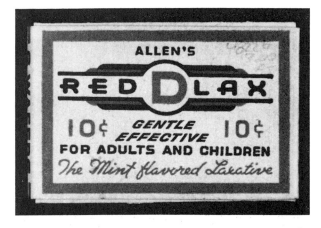

Allen's Red D Lax, distr by Red D Products Co, Cleveland, OH, "the mint flavored laxative," six wafers, ¼" × 2⅜" × 1½" red and white cardboard box with red and green letters, full box **9.00**

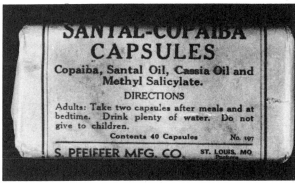

Santal-Copaiba Capsules, S. Pfeiffer Mfg Co, St. Louis, MO, packers, 40 caps, 1" × 3½" × 1½" yellow paper package (contains bottle) with red letters, full unopened sealed package **15.00**

Melcalose Tablets, Whitehall Pharmacol Co, New York, NY, USA, "for correction of constipation," 130 tabs, 4½" × 1¾" × 1¼" brown glass bottle with white metal lid in 4⅝" × 2⅛" × 1⅜" gray and maroon cardboard box with white and black letters, instruction sheet, full bottle **7.00**

Neo Probilin, Schering & Glatz, Inc, New York, St. Louis, "stimulates the flow of bile and promotes evacuation," 75 tabs, 2¾" × 1½" × 1⅛" clear glass bottle with yellow metal lid in 3¼" × 1¾" × 1¼" yellow and maroon cardboard box with maroon and yellow letters, full bottle **6.00**

NR Tablets (Nature's Remedy), The A. H. Lewis Medicine Co, St. Louis, MO, USA, Canadian office, Windsor, ONT, "acts on the stomach, liver, kidneys, and bowels," 2¾" × 2" × 1" red and blue metal container with white and black letters, empty container **10.00**

Oxiphen, Pitman-Moore Co, Div of The Dow Chemical Co, Indianapolis, IN, made in USA, "a non-toxic laxative," 1,000 tabs, 6¾" × 2¾" × 2" brown glass bottle with white metal lid, white label with blue letters, almost-empty **8.75**

Peppets, Peppet Laboratories Distr, Cincinnati, OH, USA, "pleasant chocolated laxative tablets," 150 tabs, 3¾" × 1⅝" × 1½" white plastic bottle with black plastic lid in 5¼" × 2" × 1½" blue and white cardboard box with blue letters, full bottle **6.00**

Phenolax, The Upjohn Co, Kalamazoo, MI, "a mild laxative for relief of constipation," 30 wafers, 2¼" × ¾" × ⅞" clear glass bottle with white metal lid in 2½" × 1½" × 1" gray and white cardboard box with black letters, full bottle **3.00**

Podaphen Pills, The Norwich Pharmacal Co, "soft mass laxative," 30 pills, 2½" × 1" × ¾" brown glass jar with black metal lid, gray label with red and brown letters, full jar **2.75**

Ramon's Laxative with Bile Salts, Brown Mfg Co, Distr, LeRoy, NY, 50 pills, 3″ × 1″ × 1¼″ brown glass bottle with black metal lid in 3⅛″ × 1½″ × 1⅛″ blue and white cardboard box with blue and white letters, picture of the "Little Doctor," full bottle **5.00**

Saraka, Union Pharmaceutical Co Inc, Distr, Montclair, NJ, "for constipation," 60 tabs, 3″ × 1½″ × 2″ orange and white cardboard box with black letters, instruction sheet, full box **8.50**

MISCELLANEOUS LAXATIVE PRODUCTS

Bacon's Celery King, S. C. Wells & Co, LeRoy, NY; Toronto, CAN, "an herbal laxative for constipation," 2¼-oz, 1¼″ × 2½″ × 3¾″ brown cardboard box with brown letters, full box **6.00**

Mucilose Granules, Frederick Stearns & Co, Detroit, USA, "a highly purified hemicellulose consisting of pentosans, hexosans, and galactans to afford bulk and lubrication," 4-oz, 6″ × 2½″ brown glass jar with white metal lid, gray and brown label with black letters, full jar **5.25**

Perrigo's Carm-Lax, packaged by L. Perrigo Co, Allegan, MI, "a pleasant and effective laxative," 24-piece, ⅝″ × 3¼″ × 2⅛″ purple cardboard box with purple, orange, and white letters, full box **7.50**

Ramon's Herbs, Brown Mfg Co, LeRoy, NY, "a laxative," 1½-oz, 2¾″ × 2¼″ × 1¼″ metal container, yellow and blue label with blue letters, picture of the "Little Doctor," full container **7.25**

Dr. Springer's Antediluvian Tea, Basic Foods Inc, Somerset, PA, "intestinal laxative," ¾-oz, 3″ × 2″ × ¾″ blue and white cardboard box with blue letters, picture of woman jumping, full box **12.00**

Men's Toiletries

Life in the late 1940s and the 1950s certainly was slower than it is today. Families driving on a vacation trip would look forward to those deep-red wooden signs with white lettering that appeared on the side of the road. Jingles like ' "Take it easy, take it slow, let our little shavers grow" and "Tempted to try it, follow your hunch, be top banana, not one of the bunch" meant only one thing—Burma Shave.

By the mid-1950s, many companies that produced women's toiletries began to discover a veritable gold mine in men's products.

MEN'S COLOGNE

Men's cologne, such as Seaforth, Old Spice, Currier & Ives (The J. B. Williams Company, Inc.), and By George were usually sold in masculine decanters. Scents were also packaged in milk glass decanters, brown demonstrator bottles, and aluminum-covered boxes. With the exception of Old Spice's "Burly" and Jovan's "Musk," the scents themselves were not named. They were simply called "cologne."

By George! Carl Richards, New York, "cologne for men," 4-fl oz, 5½″ × 1⅜ × 1⅜″

clear glass bottle with black plastic lid, black label with white and gold letters, full bottle **8.00**

Jovan Musk Aftershave, "cologne for men," 2-fl oz, 3¾″ × 2″ × ¾″ clear plastic bottle with silver metal lid in 5¼″ × 5⅝″ × 1½″ silver cardboard box with silver letters, bar of soap included, almost-full bottle **8.50**

Old Spice Burley, Shulton Inc, Clifton, NJ; Toronto, "cologne for men,' 4¾-fl oz, 5¾″ × 2″ brown glass bottle with pump top, gold and white letters, picture of ship, ½-full demonstrator bottle **7.00**

MEN'S DEODORANTS

Men have odors, too. In the late 1950s, companies producing feminine toiletries began to think of masculine-sounding names for men's deodorants. Mr. Fresh was "for men of action." It utilized a vaporizer system to fight underarm odor. A cloud-like spray penetrated underarm hair and put Mr. Fresh where it would do the most good.

Mennen Speed Stick Deodorant gave lasting protection against underarm odor and would not evaporate in the container. Colgate-Palmolive Co. guaranteed "Active protection . . . crisp lively scent" with its aerosol can of Tackle Spray Deodorant. Its gentle and effective formula was safe for a young adult's skin and was nonstaining.

Thirty-five years later, almost equal space is allocated to the antiperspirant needs of men.

Mr. Fresh Deodorant, Pharma-Craft Co, Batavia, IL, "stops all the perspiration it is safe to stop," 1.8-fl oz, 4″ × 1½″ × ⅞″ green plastic bottle with white plastic lid in 4″ × 2⅜″ × 1⅛″ green and white cardboard box with green, white, and yellow letters **6.00**

Stag Deodorant Cream, Langlois, Boston, Los Angeles, "sold only at Rexall Drug Stores," 1½-oz, 1¾″ × 2″ × 2″ cloudy white glass jar with tan metal lid, orange label with red and white letters, picture of a stag, full glass jar **7.50**

Tackle Spray Deodorant, Pharmaceutical Division, Colgate-Palmolive Co, distr New York, made in USA, "checks perspiration odor for 24 hours," 4-oz, 5″ × 2⅛″ metal can with gold metal lid, blue and white label with blue and white letters **5.00**

MEN'S HAIR PRODUCTS

The advent of rock and roll began to place strong emphasis on men's hairstyles and products. Cru Butch Hair Wax by Lucky Tiger, Rexall's "Mr. Groom," and Max Factor's "Crew-Cut" depicted smiling teenagers with short haircuts.

Vaseline hair tonic was a clear, cool green liquid that groomed and conditioned hair "naturally." A dandruff-fighting ingredient was eventually added to the product. Wildroot Cream-Oil came in a convenient dispenser-type bottle and was to be used daily for best results.

West Point Hair Trainer (no affiliation with the U.S. Military academy) smartly disciplined the hair but contained no alcohol to burn or grease or stain. This clean, manly fragrance was ideal for all kinds of haircuts and for men of all ages. It was so effective that only a few drops were needed to do the job!

Ayer's Hair Vigor, J. C. Ayer's Co, 7¾″ × 2⅜″ × 1⅞″ cobalt blue glass-stoppered bottle, label around small neck of bottle, name embossed on sides and bottom of bottle **45.00**

Beau Kreml Tonic, The J. B. Williams Co Inc, Toiletries Div, Cranford, NJ, "keeps hair in place neatly all day," 5-fl oz, 4″ × 2¾″ × 1½″ clear glass bottle with black plastic lid, gold label with black letters, full bottle **6.50**

Cru Butch Hair Wax, Lucky Tiger Mfg Co, Kansas City, MO, "for butch, crew, burr haircuts," 3½-oz, 2⅞″ × 2″ clear glass jar with white metal lid, white, black, and red label with white and black letters, picture of man's face, full jar **10.00**

Fitch Ideal Hair Tonic, The F. W. Fitch Division of the Grove Laboratories Inc, St. Louis, MO, "for dry hair and loose dandruff," 12-fl oz, 7½″ × 2½″ clear glass bottle with white plastic lid, yellow, black, and red label with black and white letters, full bottle **8.75**

Greasy Kid Stuff, Kid Stuff Products Inc, Chicago, IL, "for your hair," 4-fl oz, 5¼″ × 1⅞″ × 1″ clear plastic bottle with red plastic lid and squeeze spout, red letters, picture of little man, full bottle **12.00**

Lucky Cru Butch Hair-Wax Dressing, Lucky Tiger Mfg Co, Kansas City, MO, "for butch, crew, and burr haircuts," 1½-oz, 3¾″ × 1¼″ plastic container with red plastic-comb lid, blue, red, and white label with blue and white letters, picture of man's head **6.00**

Display: 12 containers, in 6¼″ × 6¼″ × 7¾″ white, blue, and red cardboard box with white and blue letters, picture of man's head, empty box **10.00**

Lucky Tiger Dandruff Treatment, Lucky Tiger Mfg Co, Kansas City, MO, printed in USA, "controls dandruff, relieves scalp itching," 4-fl oz, 5½″ × 2″ × 1½″ clear glass bottle with black plastic lid, yellow-and-white striped label with green and blue letters, full bottle **11.00**

Max Factor Crew Cut, Max Factor and Co, Hollywood, CA, "created for the control of short hair," 3-oz, 2¾″ × 2⅛″ clear glass jar with white metal lid, red and white label with black and white letters, full jar **7.00**

Moroline Hair Tonic, Moroline Co, Div of Plough Inc, New York, NY; Memphis, TN, "massage it well on to the scalp with finger tips once a day or as often as required," 4-fl oz, 6½″ × 2″ clear glass bottle with red metal lid, silver and white label with red letters, full bottle **9.25**

Mr. Groom Hair Controller, Rexall Drug Co, Los Angeles, "for butch cuts, crew cuts, regular cuts," ⅗-oz, 2¾″ × 2¼″ clear glass jar with white metal lid, black, blue, and

white label with black and white letters, full jar **8.00**

Playtex Hair Cutter, by Precision Products Div, International Latex Corp, Dover, DE, USA, and Foreign Patents Pending, printed in USA, "the home barber for the entire family," 7¼″ × ¾″ × 1″ brown clear plastic container includes 7″ × 1½″ stainless-steel cutter, double-edge blade, and cutter cleaner brush, in 7½″ × 1⅞″ × 1⅛″ white cardboard box with gold letters **18.00**

Rexall Bay Rum, Rexall Drug Co, Los Angeles, St. Louis, Toronto, printed in USA, "for external use only," 1-pt, 9¼″ × 2½″ clear glass bottle with white plastic lid, green and white label with green letters, almost-full bottle **10.00**

Tonicream Compound Hair Tonic, Pinaud World Famous since 1810, Paris, New York, Toronto, "keeps hair in place naturally, lubricates the scalp, relieves dryness," 12½-fl oz, 8¾″ × 2½″ clear glass bottle with black plastic lid, white label with black letters, picture of flowers, ½-full bottle **10.00**

Vam Hair Tonic, Colgate Palmolive Co, New York, NY, made in USA, "grooms and conditions hair," 2-fl oz, 3¾″ × 2¼″ × 1⅛″ clear glass bottle with white plastic lid in 4⅛″ × 2½″ × 1¼″ white, gold, and red cardboard box with black letters, full bottle **8.50**

Vex For The Hair, Blake Pharmacal Co, Allegan, MI, "liquid hair dressing," 8-fl oz, 2¼″ × 7¼″ round clear glass bottle, green and white label and letters, empty bottle **8.75**

West Point Hair Trainer, Associated Brands Inc, Brooklyn, NY, "smartly disciplines the hair," 1-pt, 9¼″ × 2½″ clear glass bottle with red metal lid, red and green label with black and white letters, almost-full bottle **12.00**

Wildroot Cream Oil Hair Tonic, distr by Wildroot Co Inc, Buffalo, NY, 7-fl oz, 4½″ × 2¾″ × 2¾″ clear glass bottle with white plastic pump lid, gold letters, full bottle **10.00**

Young Lad Hair Trainer and Shampoo Kit, Helene Pessl, distr, New York, NY, made in USA, "for that ship-shape look," 5" × 2" red, white, and blue tubes with white plastic lid, clear brown plastic pocket comb, 2⅓" × 4" red plastic brush in 5¼" × 1⅜" blue and white cardboard box with cellophane window, blue letters, two full tubes **18.00**

MEN'S SHAVING PRODUCTS

Early packaging of shaving products was synonymous with exotic ingredients and product claims. Huntsman Afterglow Shaving Lotion contained the soothing qualities of balsam oil and the fragrance of a virgin forest. The label on the bottle featured a hunter and his dog.

Lilac Vegetal was made in accordance with the original world-famous (since 1910) French formula. Lilac Vegetal could also be splashed freely on the body after a bath as a skin tonic. Stimulating and refreshing, it also relaxed tired muscles, relieved fatigue, and was excellent as a deodorant.

Eventually, Colgate and Mennen began producing products with newer formulas and less ornate labeling, packaging, and wording. (It was assumed that by then the customer knew what he was putting on his body!)

Men's After Shave

Colgate After Shave Lotion, Colgate-Palmolive Co, New York, 5-fl oz, 4½" × 2¼" × 1⅜" clear glass bottle with red plastic lid, red and white label with black and white letters, full bottle **7.00**

Huntsman Afterglow Shaving Lotion, Magitex Co Inc, Sago, ME, "a forest product for men who appreciate the best, combining the soothing qualities of fir balsam oil and the fragrance of virgin forests," 6-fl oz, 4¾" × 3" × 1½" clear glass bottle with black plastic lid, green and white label with black letters, picture of hunter, empty bottle **8.00**

Lilac Vegetal Aftershave Lotion, distr Ed Pinaud Inc, est. in Paris 1810, New York,

London, Paris, "soothing, excellent for tender skin, seals tiny nicks, a stimulating body freshner and refined deodorant," 6-fl oz, 6½" × 2¼" × 1¾" clear glass bottle with white plastic lid, white label with black and red letters, picture of lilacs, full sealed bottle **15.00**

Sir After Shave Lotion, Colonia Inc, New York, NY, distr, "especially for sensitive skin, just as effective after an electric shave," 1.69-fl oz, 3¾" × 2½" × 1" clear glass bottle with blue and white plastic lid, blue and black label with black and white letters, ¼-full bottle **7.25**

Men's Brushless Shaving Cream

The Colgate-Palmolive Company included directions for the *new* Palmolive brushless way to shave. Users were directed to wash face with soap and water; rinse; soap face again; do not rinse; apply Palmolive Brushless immediately and smooth it upward into the beard to get the full benefit of Palmolive Brushless' beard-conditioning effect; and finally shave, wetting razor often.

Colgate Instant Barber Shave, Colgate-Palmolive Co, New York, NY, 6¼-oz, 5⅜" × 2⅛" red and white metal container with red plastic lid over spray top, blue letters, full container **7.00**

Gillette Brushless Shaving Cream, The Gillette Co, Boston, MA, USA, "when you soften your whiskers with Gillette Shaving Cream, you enjoy the advantage of a sensational facial antiseptic K-34, 5-oz, 7" × 2" white tube with white plastic lid in 7½" × 1½" × 2¼" white cardboard box with red and blue letters, full tube **8.75**

Mollé Brushless Shaving Cream, The Centaur-Caldwell Div of Sterling Drug Inc, New York, NY, "gives you a close clean shave without pull or scrape," 8-oz, 2½" × 3¼" clear glass jar with yellow and brown metal lid in 3½" × 3½" × 2¾" yellow and brown cardboard box with white letters, full jar **10.00**

4.5-oz, 6½" × 1¾" tube, full tube **8.00**

Noxema Brushless Shave Cream, Noxema Chemical Co, Baltimore, MD, 10-oz, 2¾″ × 3″ cobalt blue glass jar, full jar **8.00**

Palmolive Brushless Shaving Cream, Colgate-Palmolive Co, Jersey City, NJ, 2⅜-oz, 5″ × 1¾″ white tube with green plastic lid in 5½″ × 1¼″ × 1⅝″ green and white cardboard box with white, green, and red letters, full tube **10.00**

Prep Medicated Brushless Deluxe Shave, Mark Allen Co, Detroit, MI, USA, "helps bring prompt relief from sunburn, minor burns, insect bites, chapped skin, foot discomforts, stops razor burns and nicks," ⅘-oz, 2½″ × 2¼″ red and white plastic jar with red metal lid, red and white letters, full jar **6.50**

Stag Electric Pre-Shave Lotion, Rexall Drug Co, Los Angeles, "apply on beard before using electric razor," 3-fl oz, 4½″ × 2½″ × 1″ clear glass bottle with gold metal lid in 4¾″ × 2¾″ × 1¼″ white, green, and gray cardboard box with green and gold letters, pictures of stags, full bottle **11.00**

Yardley Shaving Cream, makers & distr for USA, Yardley of London, Inc, New York, "immediately produces an abundant fine-textured lather, its use ensures a clean rapid easy shave with your skin left cool and comfortable," 2.8-oz, 5½″ × 2″ tube with white plastic lid in green, white, and black cardboard box with white, green, and black letters, full tube **8.50**

Men's Razor Blades

From large companies such as Gillette to smaller companies such as Laymon's in Spencer, Indiana, the razor blade business was quite diverse. Pal Hollow-Ground blade (like your barber's razor) proclaimed itself to be "the greatest improvement since the invention of the safety razor." Now it was possible to give yourself a master barber's shave with your own safety razor!

Many of the blades were made from Swedish steel and were carefully inspected. Satisfaction was guaranteed or money would gladly be refunded.

Of the twenty items in this section, only "Pal" blades fit all types of injection razors.

Berkeley Double Edge Blades, mfr by Consolidated Razor Blake Co Inc, Jersey City, NJ, four blades, in 2″ × 1″ × ¼″ red and black cardboard box with white letters, full box **2.00**

Double-Edge Purple Blades, Purple Blade Corp, San Francisco, CA, ten blades in 2″ × 1″ × ⅜″ purple and white cardboard box with white and purple letters, full box **2.50**

Ever-Ready "Radio" Steel Safety Razor Blade, American Safety Razor Corp, Brooklyn, NY, made in USA, 1½″ × ⅞″ × 1/16″ blade wrapped in blue and white paper with blue and white letters, picture of man shaving **6.00**

Gillette Blue Blades, Gillette Safety Razor Co, Boston, MA, five blades in 1⅞″ × 1″ × ¼″ blue and white cardboard box with black letters, picture of King Gillette (man), full box **2.50**

Gold Tone Master Action Single Edge Blades, mfr and guaranteed by Gold Tone Razor Blade Co, Newark, NJ, four blades in 2″ × 1″ × ¼″ gold and brown cardboard box with brown letters, full box **4.00**

Hospital Razor Blade, Hospital Blade Co, Newark, NJ, 1¾″ × 1″ × 1/16″ blade wrapped in green and white paper with green and white letters **3.00**

Keen Kutter Double Edge Blades, Shapleigh Hardware Co, St. Louis, MO, USA, five blades in 2″ × 1″ × ¼″ green and white cardboard box with green, white, and red letters, full unopened cellophane-wrapped box **7.50**

Laymon's Razor Blades, owners and distr World's Products Co, Spencer, IN, USA, five blades in 1⅞″ × 1″ × ¼″ orange, blue, and white cardboard box with blue and white letters, picture of man shaving, full box **4.50**

Majestic Razor blades, made in USA, four single-edged blades in 1¾″ × 1″ × ⅝″ yellow, white, and blue cardboard box with blue and white letters **3.25**

Harmony Blades, Harmony Razor Blade Co, New York, Chicago, five blades in 2″ × 1⅛″ × ¼″ in red and blue cardboard box with white letters, full box **3.50**

Pal Hollow Ground Blade, mfr by Pal Blade Co, New York, made in USA, 1⅞″ × 1″ × ¹⁄₁₆″ blade in blue and white paper with white letters on 4″ × 2¾″ blue and white display card with blue and white letters, picture of man **9.00**

Pal Injector Blades, Precision ASR Products, ASR Products Corp, New York, NY, 20 blades, 3″ × ¾″ × ⅜″ metal injector in 3⅜″ × ⅞″ × ¾″ white, red, and blue cardboard box with white letters **5.00**

Probak Blades, guaranteed by Probak Div Gillette Safety Razor Co, five blades in 1⅞″ × 1″ × ¼″ red, blue, white, and green cardboard box with white letters, full unopened box **3.25**

Rex Super Stainless Steel Blades, Rexall Drug Co, distr, Los Angeles, Toronto, London, ten blades in 2⅜″ × 1¼″ × ½″ plastic dispenser in 2½″ × 1¼″ × ½″ red, white, and gray cardboard box with black and white letters, full unopened cellophane-wrapped box **3.50**

Shelby Ultra Thin, mfr and guaranteed by Federal Razor Blade Co, New York, 2″ × 1″ × ¼″ green and blue cardboard box with blue letters, partly full **4.00**

Smith Blades, Smith & Smith Inc, New York, NY, USA, four blades in 2″ × 1″ × ¼″ orange and blue cardboard box with blue and white letters, full box **3.00**

Treet Blades, Treet Safety Razor Corp, Brooklyn, NY, made in USA, three blades in 1⅛″ × 1¾″ × ⅜″ red, blue, and yellow cardboard box with white letters, full box **4.25**

Display: 12½″ × 9⅛″ red, yellow, and blue cardboard stand with white, yellow, and blue letters, holds 20 boxes **100.00**

Twenty Grand Double-Edge Blades, Twenty Grand Blade Co, Spencer, IN, USA, five blades in 2″ × 1″ × ¼″ blue, red, and white cardboard box with blue and white letters, picture of a jockey on horse, partly-full box **5.00**

Utility Blade, Utility Blade Corp, Maplewood, NJ, 1⅞″ × 1″ × ¹⁄₁₆″ blade wrapped in orange, blue, and gold paper with gold letters **5.00**

Valet Auto Strop Blades, Autostrop Div, The Gillette Co, Boston, MA, USA, five blades in 1⅞″ × 1″ × ¼″ red and white cardboard box with red and white letters, full unopened cellophane-wrapped box **4.25**

Waltham, A Precision Blade, Waltham Blade Co, Newark, NJ, five blades in 2″ × 1″ × ¼″ light and dark blue cardboard box with blue and white letters, full box **2.50**

Men's Razors

Men's Razors came in a variety of styles, materials, and colors. One unique razor was the Keen Cutter Razor, which had a green celluloid handle and was manufactured by a company that also made tools. The Christy Safety Razor with the Massage Bar "Keeps Your Face Young." (The massage bar was complimentary with the purchase of the razor.) The Gem "Minute Man" had a convenient dispenser that could be placed on the shelf or hung on the wall. The Shick Instamatic Razor had a ten-edged band cartridge, and the Lord Sheffield Disposable Razor with super stainless-steel blades provided shaving efficiency.

Christy Safety Razor with the Massage Bar, The Christy Sales Co, Fremont, OH, "ease and comfort in shaving are aided by the fact that every blade is hand stropped, individually tested, and made especially for Christy Razor with the massage bar," 4¼″ × 1½″ × ¾″ metal razor in 4¼″ × 1¾″ × ¾″ blue cardboard box with red and white letters. "This Christy Razor with the massage bar is not to be sold. It is complimentary, presented for demonstration with Christy Blades" **15.00**

Clippers, O.V.C. Co, made in USA, 5″ × 1½″ × 1½″ metal beard clipper with squeeze handle **15.00**

Durham-Demonstrator, Durham Duplex Razor Co, New York, London, Toronto, Berlin, made in USA, "a working model of the $5 Durham Duplex Razor," 8¼″ × 1⅛″ × ¼″ metal fold-up razor with black plastic handle in 6⅛″ × 1½″ × ¾″ brown cardboard box, red label with gold letters **6.00**

Eversharp-Schick Injector Razor, Eversharp Inc, Bridgeport, CT, 3¾″ × 1½″ × ½″ gold metal razor with white injector in 4¾″ × 2½″ × 1″ red plastic box with clear flip-top lid, clear letters **10.00**

Display: 6¼″ × 5¼″ × 2¾″ red metal rack with attached 6¼″ × 5″ red and yellow cardboard flap with white, black, and yellow letters, in 6½″ × 5¼″ × 3″ brown cardboard box with red letters, picture of the razor, holds six kits, display alone **15.00**
Full **75.00**

Gillette Razor, made in USA, 2¾″ × 1¾″ × ¾″ metal razor with designed metal handle **4.00**

3½″ × 1⅝″ × 1″ metal razor with black plastic grip **6.00**

Keen Kutter Razor, made in USA, 4″ × 1⅝″ × ⅝″ metal razor with green plastic handle **14.00**

Lord Sheffield Disposable Razor, Intermark Corp, "the lightest touch in shaving today, a week of shaves, then throw it away," 3″ × 1⅞″ × 1″ blue plastic razor in 3″ × 1⅞″ × 1″ blue-and-black striped cardboard box with cellophane window, black letters **8.00**

Star Safety Razor, made by Kampfe Bros., New York, USA, 2¼″ × 1⅜″ yellow and black metal container with black letters, picture of a man shaving **65.00**

MEN'S TALCUM

Old Spice by Shulton did its best to corner the market for men's toiletries. For talcum powders alone, there was a body talc in a red plastic container with gold top, a nautical talc in a milk glass bottle with the ship "Mount Vernon" depicted on the label, and elaborately boxed lime body talc complete with corrugated plastic container and unique shaker top.

Colonial Club Powder for Men, Nelson-Detroit, Inc, distributors, Detroit, MI, 3-oz, 5″ × 2½″ × 1¼″ metal container with shaker top, yellow and brown label with brown and white letters, picture of colonial man, full container **15.00**

Old Spice Lime Body Talc, Shulton Inc, Clifton, NJ, 5½-oz, 4½″ × 3¼″ × 1⅜″ white plastic container with shaker top in a 4½″ × 3½″ × 1½″ green cardboard box with white letters and window, full container **10.00**

Tally-Ho, Tally-Ho Distributor, Fifth Avenue Building, New York, NY, 3-oz, 3½″ × 2⅝″ × 1″ yellow metal container with metal lid over shaker top, brown letters and picture of horses pulling a stagecoach with a group of men, full container **10.00**

MISCELLANEOUS MEN'S TOILETRIES

"Snow" was a facial depilatory powder that removed hair and beard painlessly from one's face and legs. This concoction was deodorized, quick, and economical.

A lucky man could expect a festive light plastic stocking filled with a variety of Williams products, including talc and after-shave cream. A seasoned business traveler could pack an assortment of Tawn products intricately placed in a handy heavy plastic case. It would fold up to two-thirds of its fold-out size and be secured with a maroon cord.

The Curtiss Candy Company of Chicago invented Spee-D-Hone, a device that sharpened double-edged razor blades. It took only a minute to use, and the customer could save up to $10 a year on razor blades.

Styptic Products Company of Glendale, California, included the "Before" and "After" of "Butch the Careless Shaver" in every full display box. Before Butch used this convenient product, his face was covered with small cuts and nicks. The "After" Butch had a clean and shining face because he had used these effective and inexpensive sticks (32 for 10¢).

Chex-it Styptic Sticks, made in USA, Styptic Products Co, Glendale, CA, "stops bleeding of small cuts and scratches," 32 sticks, 2⅞" × 1⅞" × ¼" yellow booklet with black letters **2.00**

Display: 6⅛" × 3¾" × 2⅛" white cardboard box with red lid, black and white fold-up advertising flap with black, white, and red letters, holds 26 booklets, display alone **7.00** full 26 booklets **64.00**

Electric Razor Cleaning Brushes, "cleans all electric shavers," 3¼" × 4" wire and bristle brushes, on 5" × 3½" yellow card with black letters, two brushes **5.00**

Gift Stocking, The J. B. Williams Co, Glastonbury, CT, USA, "shaving supplies," clear plastic 4¼" × 11" stocking; contents: talc, razor, blades, shaving cream, and after shave, pictures of holly and bells, full unopened stocking **45.00**

Gillette Display Case, Gillette Safety Razor Co, Boston, MA, 12" × 17½" × 2½" white and blue plastic box with glass flip-up lid, blue letters **65.00**

Red Magic Shaving Powder, Carson Chemical Co, Savannah, GA, "extra strength depilatory which removes beard without razor, 1966," 5-oz, 2" × 4¼" red and white cardboard cylinder, full **8.50**

Remington Speedak, a product of Remington Rand Electric Shaver, Div of Sperry Rand Corp, Bridgeport, CT, "makes every shave a faster shave, gives old shavers new life, increases voltage, speed up shaver, extra power for extra tough beards," 2" × 1⅜" × 3" plastic adapter plug in 5¼" × 3½" × 1½" black cardboard box with cellophane lid, yellow, brown, and gold label with black letters **9.00**

Schick World Traveler's Kit, "adapts American volt shavers to foreign voltages," black Bakelite adapter and plugs in 4½" × 3½" × 2" maroon box **30.00**

Shaverest for Schick Shavers, designed and produced by W. L. Stensgard & Associates, Inc, Chicago, New York, Oakland, "keeps shaver finger-tip handy by your bathroom mirror, holds it safely, current shuts off automatically, built-in cord reel zips up the cord, for use with any Shick Shaver," 7¾" × 12" × 5½" wooden stand with black plastic shaver holder, plug and electric cord, gold and red letters **90.00**

Shaving Brush, Erskine 3¼" × 1⅜" red plastic handle with animal-hair bristles **5.50**

Snow, Rasofix Corp of America, New York, NY, "facial depilatory, removes hair and beard from face or limbs painlessly, without razor or pulling, deodorized, quick, economical," powder, in 6" × 2" light blue and black cardboard cylinder, tin top and bottom with black and white letters, picture of man and woman who used the "Snow," full cylinder **40.00**

Spee-D-Hone, mfr by Curtiss Candy Co, Chicago, IL, "sharpens double-edge razor blades," 3¾" × 3" × ¾" yellow, red, white, and blue cardboard box with white, blue, and red letters, picture of man sharpening razor **8.00**

Sunbeam Comb and Blade for Shavemaster Razor, Sunbeam Corp, Chicago, IL, made in USA, "for models 140, 140L, G. W.," 2¼″ × 1¼″ metal and cardboard container with metal lid, gray, black, and red label with black and white letters, instruction sheet **5.50**

Sunbeam Comb and Cutter for Shavemaster Model's, Sunbeam Corp, Chicago, IL, made in USA, 1⅜″ × 1¼″ metal and cardboard container, gray and red label with red and gray letters **5.00**

Tawn Men's Travel Kit, mfr by McKesson & Robbins Inc, New York, Bridgeport, "toiletry supplies," 7″ × 15″ red plastic hanging kit with pockets. Contents: pocket comb, razor blades, four ½-fl oz glass bottles, shampoo, cologne, hair dressing, lotion, two ¾-oz tins, tooth powder, talc, one ¾-oz tube of brushless shave, gold letters **38.00**

Nasal Products

One early nasal product was 'Mistol," manufactured by the Standard Oil Company in a cork-stoppered, embossed glass bottle. Glycol Thymoline was an alkaline cleansing solution that soothed the skin and mucous membranes around the nasal passages. Kondon's Nasal Jelly was inserted into the nostrils to relieve stuffiness. Neo-Synephrine offered fast, penetrating relief from nasal congestion resulting from head colds and hay fever.

Glyco Thyoline, Kress & Owen Co, New York, NY, "an alkaline, deodorizing and non-irritating solution for application to skin and mucous membranes," 6-fl oz square clear glass embossed bottle in 4¾″ × 2¾″ × 2⅜″ orange, black, and gold box with black and gold letters, ½-full bottle **10.00**

Hart's Efemist Inhalant, Hart Drug Corp, Miami, FL, USA, "reduces congestion of nose and throat," 1-fl oz round glass bottle in 3½″ × 1⅜″ × 1⅜″ black and light green box with black and white letters, dropper and folder included, ½-full bottle **6.00**

Hill's Nose Drops, Wyeth Chemical Co, Distr Jersey City, NJ, "relief of nasal congestion, ½-fl oz green bottle with green metal cap in 1¾″ × 3¼″ × 1⅜″ green and yellow box with green and yellow stripes and letters, dropper and folder included, full bottle **5.00**

Holford's Famous Inhaler, Holford's, Minneapolis, MN, Distr by C. R. Maloney & Son, Corbin, KY, 2⅜″ × ⅝″ cork-stoppered glass cylinder with gold, black, and red graphics, empty cylinder **4.75**

Kondon's Nasal Jelly, Kondon Mfg Co, Minneapolis, MN, 1⅛-oz plastic squeeze tube with picture of small girl in 5⅜″ × 1⅜″ × 1¼″ blue, red, and white box, with T. N. Kenyon signature, originated by T. N. Kenyon, 1889, almost-full tube **10.00**

Mistol Nose & Throat Spray, Nujol Laboratories, Standard Oil Co, Bayonne, NJ, USA, 4-fl oz clear glass "Mistol" embossed bottle, tan label with black and orange letters, ¾-full bottle **12.00**

Nasal Drops, L. Perrigo Co, Allegan, MI, "for nose and throat irritations," 1-fl oz, 3½″ × 1½″ glass bottle with metal cap, two-tone blue, black, and white label with blue and white letters, full bottle **6.50**

Neo-Synephrine, North Brook Prescriptions, Richmond, IN, "temporary relief of nasal congestion," 3⅞″ × 1⅝″ green bottle with stopper top, ¼-full bottle **3.75**

Rexall Aqueous Nose Drops, Rexall Drug Co, Los Angeles, Boston, St. Louis, USA; Toronto, CAN, "relief of congestion and nose irritation," brown bottle with white metal cap and white dropper in 3¾″ × 2½″ × 1″ pale blue, dark blue, and white box with dark blue letters, ¼-full bottle **8.00**

Rexall Nasal'ator Inhaler, Rexall Drug Co, Los Angeles, Toronto, "relieves nasal congestion," 2½″ × ¾″ white plastic cylinder with blue letters **5.00**

Rexall Vapure, Rexall Drug Co, Los Angeles, Boston, St. Louis, "relief of minor bronchial and nasal irritations," 1-fl oz glass

Bayer Nasal Spray, The Bayer Co, Div of Sterling Drug Inc, New York, NY, "fast nasal congestion relief," 1" × 3⅛" plastic squeeze cylinder, empty cylinder **6.50**

Efedron Nasal Jelly, Hart Laboratories Inc, Paoli, PA, "congestion relief," 20-gram aluminum tube with white, green, and yellow graphics, in 4⅝" × ¾" × 1" dark green and white box with dark green and white letters, almost-full tube **5.00**

bottle in 3½" × 1¾" × 1" dark blue, light blue, and white box with blue and white letters, full bottle **3.25**

Vapex Inhalant, E. Fougerad Co Inc, Hicksville, NY, "helps relieve head colds and nasal stuffiness," ½-fl oz bottle in 2⅛" × 1⅛" × 1" green and white box with black letters, picture of a woman, folder included, full bottle **6.00**

Pharmacy Reference Books

Some physicians, pharmacists, chemists, and others in the field of health collect the PDR (*Physician's Desk Reference*). Collectors find it a challenge to locate a complete set in mint condition. Medical directories for major cities, chemical company price schedules, dose books, and National Formularies are equally desirable. (**Collecting hint:** Hospital auxiliary tag sales, liquidation sales of chemical companies, auctions of physicians' or pharmacists' estates, and used book stores are excellent sources for additional volumes.)

Abbott Pharmaceuticals General Catalog, Abbott Laboratories, North Chicago, IL, 161 pages, 6½" × 8" × 1½", hardcover, illustrated **15.00**

American Drug Index, 1957, Charles O. Wilson, Ph.D., and Tony Everett Jones, M.S., J. B. Lippincott Co, Philadelphia and Montreal, 650 pages, 8¼" × 5½" × 1½", hardcover **10.00**

1959, 671 pages **10.00**

The Dispensatory of the United States of America, Twenty-fifth edition, Arthur Osol, PH.G.B.S., M.S., Ph.D., and George E. Farrar, Jr, B.S., M.D., F.A.C.P., J. B. Lippincott Co, Philadelphia and Montreal, two volumes in one book 1960, 2,379 pages, hardcover **9.00**

An Encyclopedia of Practical Information and Universal Formulary, John E. Potter &

Co, Philadelphia, *A Book of Ready Reference for Every Occupation, Trade and Profession,* by Robert Bradbury, M.D., eight volumes in one, 1888, 779 pages, 8″ × 10″ × 3″, hardcover **15.00**

Dose Book, Lloyd Brothers, Cincinnati, OH, 1921, "maximum and minimum doses of specific medicines of fine medicinal specialties, their history, qualities, characteristics, therapeutic uses," lists medicines manufactured by Lloyd Brothers, 304 pages, 3⅛″ × 6¾″ × ½″, tan and black book with black letters **15.00**

Medical Directory of Greater Cincinnati, Edition VII, 1960–61, Academy of Medicine of Cincinnati; Medical Foundation Building, Cincinnati, OH, 6½″ × 8¾″ × 1″, soft cover **10.00**

Modern Drug Encyclopedia and Therapeutic Index, Edited by Edwin P. Jordan, M.D., F.A.C.P., Seventh Edition, 1958, Drug Publications Inc, New York, NY, 1,516 pages, 6¼″ × 9¼″ × 2¾″, hardcover **10.00**

The National Formulary, Ninth Edition, National Formulary IX, prepared by the Committee on National Formulary under the supervision of the Council by Authority of the American Pharmaceutical Association, Official from November 1, 1950, published by The American Pharmaceutical Association, Washington, DC, 877 pages, 6¼″ × 9¼″ × 2″, hardcover **12.00**

New and Nonofficial Remedies, containing descriptions of drugs evaluated by the Council on Pharmacy and Chemistry of the American Medical Association, 1956. An annual publication issued under the direction and supervision of the council, J. B. Lippincott Co, Philadelphia and Montreal, 540 pages, 5¼″ × 7½″ × 1¼″, hardcover **11.00**

Pfizer Laboratories Price Schedule, January 5, 1954, Pfizer Laboratories, Division, Chas. Pfizer & Co Inc, Brooklyn, NY, 7″ × 9″ × ½″, hardcover, illustrated **12.00**

Pharmacopoeia of the United States of America, Eleventh Decennial Revision (U.S.P. XI), by the authority of the United States Pharmacopoeial Convention prepared by the Committee of Revision and

Published by the Board of Trustees, official from June 1, 1936, Agent, Mack Printing Company, Easton, PA, 676 pages, 6″ × 9⅜″ × 2″ hardcover **15.00**

Physician's Desk References to Pharmaceutical Specialties and Biologicals, 1952, Sixth Edition, five sections, Section I (pink) alphabetical index of brands and manufacturers; Section II (yellow) drug, chemical, and pharmacological index; Section III (blue) therapeutic indications index; Section IV (white) professional products information; Section V (green) general professional information, J. Morgan Jones, Editor and Publisher, published by Medical Economics, Inc, Rutherford, NJ, Copyright 1951 by Medical Economics, Inc, printed in USA, pages 101–632, 7¼″ × 10¼″ × 1¼″, hardcover **10.00**

1958 Twelfth Edition, five sections, J. Paul Folsom, General Manager, published by Medical Economics, Inc, Oradell, NJ, Copyright 1957 by Medical Economics, Inc, all rights reserved, printed in USA, pages 101–949, 10¼″ × 7¼″ × 1″, hardcover **15.00**

Quantitative Pharmaceutical Chemistry, containing Theory and Practice of Quantitative Analysis applied to Pharmacy, by Glenn L. Jenkins, Ph.D., and Andrew G. Du Mez, Ph.D., Second Edition, Eleventh Impression, McGraw-Hill Book Company, Inc, New York and London, 1937, 466 pages, 3¾″ × 8¼″ × ¾″, hard cover **12.00**

Synopsis of Material Medical, Toxicology, and Pharmacology, for students and practitioners of medicine, by Forrest Ramon Davison, B.A., M.SC., Ph.D, M.B., The C.V. Mosby Company, St. Louis, Third Edition, 1944, 40 illustrations, including four in color, 759 pages, 5″ × 7¾″ × 1¼″, hardcover **12.75**

Prophylactic Items

The recent rise in cases of sexually transmitted diseases has led to an increased interest in prophylactic items. Pre-1930 tins with intricate graphics are the most sought after. A collector is indeed fortunate to locate one of the vintage vending machines that matches a specific tin. (**Collecting hint:** At present, this is one of the most popular pharmaceutical collectibles. Locating a matching tin and vending machine will evoke envy from fellow collectors!)

Sheik, Esquire, The Gold Trojan, Ramses, Guardian, and other masculine logos appeared on many of the products. "The Three Widows," "Naturalamb," and "Peacock" were more subdued names. Speculation remains as to why the National Hygienics Products Corporation named its product "Roger (OK)."

The Youngs Rubber Corporation claimed a natural animal membrane, expertly processed for maximum security. One product noted that the "kling tite" elastic top clings "snugly."

Most prophylactics were sold by pharmacists.

Esquire Rubber Prophylactics, mfr by Julius Schmid Inc, New York, NY, made in USA, "sold in drug stores only for protection against disease," 2¼" × 2¼" × ½" blue and white cardboard box containing three blue and white cellophane-sealed prophylactics, red and white letters, full box **10.00**

The Gold Trojan, Youngs Rubber Corp, Sole Distributor, New York, NY, manufacturer Trenton, NJ, made in USA, 2" × ¾" × ⅝" purple, gold and lavender cardboard box with black letters, three prophylactics **8.00**

Display: 2¼" × 3" × ¾" lavender, blue, white, and gold cardboard box with gold, blue, and lavender letters, holds one dozen prophylactics, display box alone **15.00**

Guardian Extra Sensitive Rolled Latex Prophylactics, Youngs Rubber Corp, mfr, Trenton, NJ, sole distributor, New York, NY, 2¼" × 2¼" silver and white cellophane envelope with black letters, twelve envelopes in 4⅝" × 2¼" × 1" white and gray cardboard box with black letters, full box **8.00**

"Naturalamb" Skins, Sole Distributor, Young Rubber Corp, New York, NY, "made from natural animal membrane expertly processed for maximum sensitivity," 2½" × 1½" green and white paper envelope with black and green letters, nine envelopes in 6¼" × ⅝" × 2¾" green and white cardboard box with green and black letters, picture of lamb, each envelope **8.50**

Empty box **10.00**

Full box of nine **86.50**

Peacock Reservoir Ends, Dean Rubber Co, North Kansas City, MO, 2¼" × 1⅞" × ¾" yellow metal clip with red and green letters, picture of a peacock **45.00**

Polar Bears, Sterling Rubber Co, Cincinnati, OH, red, black, and white individual package with black and white letters, polar bear on front, cellophane-sealed package **22.00**

Ramses Rolled Rubber Prophylactics, mfr by Julius Schmid, Inc, New York, NY, three-pack, 2⅛" × 2⅛" × ⅝" yellow and black cardboard box with red, gold, and black letters, full plastic-sealed box **10.00**

Rogers (OK) Prophylactics, made exclusively for Roger Rubber Products, Los Angeles, by National Hygienic Products Corp, New York City, three 2½" × 1¾" red cello phane-sealed prophylactics in 2¾" × 2" × ½" red, white, and blue cardboard box with red and white letters, full box **15.00**

Display: 4" × 2¾" × 1⅛" red, white, and blue cardboard holder, holds four three-packs, Full display **66.00**

Display alone **6.00**

Sheik Rubber Prophylactics, mfr by Julius Schmid, Inc, New York, NY, made in USA, three 2¾" × 1" brown cellophane-wrapped prophylactics in 2¾" × 1¼" × ½" brown and white cardboard box with brown and white letters, full box **9.00**

Sheik with Special Dry Sensi-Creme Lubricant Rubber Prophylactic, mfr by Julius Schmid Inc, New York, NY, 2¼" × 2⅛" white cellophane package with red letters **2.00**

Trojan-Enz, manufactured in USA, Youngs Rubber Corp, mfr, sole distributor, Trenton, NJ; New York, NY, "for those who wish a special end as a receptacle," three-pack 2¾" × 1¼" × ½" white cardboard box with red and black letters **6.00**

Trojan-Enz Lubricated Rubber Prophylactic, Youngs Rubber Corp, mfr, Trenton, NJ, sole distributor, New York, NY, 2⅛" × 2⅛" blue and white cellophane package with black letters **3.00**

Trojan "Natural Lamb" Rolled Wet Skin, "This Trojan Naturalamb Wet Skin is offered by your pharmacist so you may try the new revolutionary type of prophylactic made of natural membrane," professional sample, 2½" × 2½" green and white paper envelope with black letters **4.00**

Rectal Products

Graphic descriptions were often employed when manufacturers promoted rectal medications. The F. A. Stuart Company of Marshall, Michigan, distributed Pyramid Suppositories, Gentz Wipes were "Man Size," and the Norwich Pharmaceutical Company distributed an 8-Day Treatment for the relief of itching, burning, and soreness of hemmorhoids. Chinaroid Rectal Balm was also useful for alleviating the discomfort of minor burns, cuts, sunburn, and minor skin abrasions or externally caused irritations or inflammations.

Chinaroid Rectal Balm, The Knox Co, Los Angeles, CA, "relief of irritation, itching, and pain," tube of balm with rubber cap, key to wind up end of tube, in 6" × 1½" × 1¼" yellow and navy blue box, almost-full tube **6.00**

8-Day Treatment, The Norwich Pharmaceutical Co, Norwich, NY, "relieves itching, burning, soreness of hemorrhoids," twelve cellophane-sealed suppositories plus 1-pt bottle of "Norola" liquid laxative, all in 3⅜" × 3⅜" × 10" red, black, and yellow box

with black and yellow letters, picture of contents on back of box, two packs of suppositories and one full bottle of "Norola" **38.00**

Empty Capsules for Rectal Administration of Medication, Parke-Davis & Co, Detroit, MI, USA, three sizes empty capsules in 4⅛" × 3" × 1⅜" gold and gray slide-top box with black letters, partially full box **5.00**

Gentz Wipes, Philips Roxane Laboratories, Columbus, OH, "relief of itching and discomfort, rectal cleansing," seven "man-size" foil packets in 3⅝" × 2⅛" × 1⅛" black, tan, and wine box with black, tan, and wine letters, lion shield, four pictures of different men, full box **10.00**

Lorophyn Suppositories, Eaton Laboratories, Div of The Norwich Pharmaceutical Co, Norwich, NY, twelve suppositories in 2½" × 3⅛" × 1⅝" white and pink box, cellophane wrapped **6.50**

Merrell's Suppository Machine, Pat'd, no address, "makes suppositories," round wooden holder with top, 4" × 1½" steel suppository, no instructions **40.00**

Paz-Pile Ointment, Grove Laboratories, Inc, St. Louis, MO, "relief of simple piles," 1-oz tin of ointment in 2⅛" × 2⅛" × ⅞" red and white box with red and white letters, folder **4.00**

Pyramid Suppositories, F. A. Stuart Co, Marshall, MI, "relief of minor rectal irritation," twelve suppositories in 2⅝" × 1⅞" × 1½" yellow box with black letters, full box **7.50**

Rectal-Eze Ointment, Larré Laboratories, Denver, CO, "relief and treatment of hemorrhoids, piles, internal and external bleeding," six cellophane-sealed collapsible tubes in 3¼" × 2½" × ⅝" gold and black box with red and black letters, full box **8.75**

Rectalgan, Mallon Div, Doho Chem Corp, New York, NY, "hemorrhoid relief," 55-cc, 1⅜" × 1⅜" × 3¾" square blue bottle with metal cap, 3⅞" × 2¼" × 1½" tan and blue box with tan and blue letters, plastic and rubber applicator enclosed, full bottle **8.50**

Rectal Medicone, Medicone Co, New York, NY, "relief of rectal discomfort," twelve suppositories in 5⅜" × 1⅞" × ½" tan and red box with tan and red letters, full box **12.00**

Thornton Minor Rectal Ointment, Thornton Minor Clinic, Kansas City, MO, "relief of irritations, itching and pain of piles," tube of cream in 5″ × 1½″ × 1″ dark blue and tan box with dark blue letters, instruction folder included, full tube **8.00**

Reducing Aids

The early 1960s saw the proliferation of all sorts of products that encouraged weight loss. One couple was stymied as to why they were unable to lose weight when drinking liquid Metrecal—that is, until they realized they were drinking it as a prelude to a regular meal!

Eda's dietetic Hard Candies were considered safe for the teeth and were non-cariogenic (tooth decay is not promoted). Slim Vims revolutionized weight-loss strategies for men and women. Appetite-curbing cubes of candy (thirty-five calories per piece) in an assortment of flavors discouraged the palate. And Sweet'n-ets Sugar Substitute contained an increasingly popular ingredient—Saccharin!

Eda's Hard Candies, LeMan Dietetic Confections, Inc, Brooklyn, NY, USA, "lemon flavor hard candies for sugar and salt restricted diets," ¾-oz, 3¾″ × 2″ × ¾″ white, blue, and yellow box with blue, black, and white letters, picture of lemon and cherries, individually wrapped candies, full box **9.00**

Feather Weight Peppermint Drops, Chicago Dietetic Supply House Inc, Chicago, IL, USA, "candy substitute in sugar and calorie restricted diets," 2-oz green peppermint drops in 3⅜″ × 2⅜″ × ¾″ tan and white box with navy and light blue letters, picture of yellow feather, full box **9.00**

Metrecal, Mead Johnson & Co, Evansville, IN, "weight control," 8-oz, plain powder,

gold and white can with wine letters, key opener, full can **6.75**

Full butterscotch powder can **6.75**

Slim Vims-Vitamin & Mineral Candy, Paul E. Beich Co, Bloomington, IL, "helps you lose weight by depressing the appetite, chocolate fudge," 2⅝″ × 10¾″ × 1⅝″ brown, white, and blue box with brown, blue, and white letters, picture of woman and candy cubes, empty box **6.75**

Swan Saccharin Tabs, Cumberland Mfg Co, Nashville, TN, "sugar substitute for those on sugar restricted diets," 100 tabs, 2⅛″ × 1¼″ × ½″ clear bottle, full bottle **3.00**

Sweet'n-ets Sugar Sub, Rexall Drug Co, Los Angeles, Boston, St. Louis, USA, "contains saccharin," 4¼″ × 2″ octagonal glass jar with shaker top, pink and navy label with white, pink, and navy letters, full jar **8.00**

Rheumatism Remedies

Pabasone was designed to relieve the aches and pains of rheumatism, arthritis, neuritis, bursitis, and similar afflictions. Pabasone was also recommended for headaches and dysmenorrhea and was considered far superior to products containing aspirin. The red pills measured one-eighth of an inch in diameter. The special curative power of Alpha-Tablets was derived from alfalfa. Tysmol Tablets were promoted as the most healthful because they contained no narcotics, coal tar products, or bromides.

Alpha-Tablets, Wolverine Laboratories, Detroit, MI, "pain relief for arthritis and rheumatism," 100 tabs, 3⅞″ × 1″ × 1⅝″ brown bottle, yellow and green label with green and white letters, full bottle **5.50**

Beta-Sal, Todd-Dickson Pharmaceuticals, New York, NY, "relieves pain rheumatism and arthritis," 4″ × 1¾″ × 1″ brown bottle, full bottle **4.75**

Imdrin, Rhodes Pharmacal Co Inc, Chicago, IL, "pain relief for arthritis rheumatism" 30 tabs, 2½″ × 1½″ brown bottle, full bottle **6.50**

Pabasone, Pabasone Div, The Pinex Co Inc, Fort Wayne, IN, "for arthritis, rheumatism, and other pains," 100 tabs, bottle boxed with blue and white graphics, folder enclosed, full bottle **11.00**

Rumarub, S. Pfeiffer Mfg Co, St. Louis, MO, "relief of rheumatism and other aches and pains," 5-fl oz clear glass bottle, 7⅛″ × 3″ × 1¾″ tan, wine, and gold box with blue, tan, and white letters, full bottle **6.50**

Sanforin, Kedvale Pharmacal Co Inc, Chicago, IL, "rheumatism pain relief," 72 tabs, brown bottle in 4⅛″ × 1¾″ × 1¼″ mauve and white box with white and wine letters, full bottle **6.25**

Tysmol Tablets, Tysmol Co, San Francisco, CA, "pain relief for rheumatism," 100 tabs, 4″ × 1¼″ × 1¼″ tan box with red and green letters, full unopened box **6.25**

Rubs, Liniments, and Ointments

Some liniments and ointments had a single use, while others could be used for a variety of ailments. Ramon's Rub was designed for the common cold. Runion's White Wonder Salve was considered "A Doctor's Prescription" because one small bottle of ointment could be used for a variety of purposes, including colds and sunburn. Subcategories for these medications include (1) cough and cold, (2) muscular and rheumatism, (3) skin, (4) throat, and (5) general.

Waite's Green Mountain Salve was a reliable treatment for relieving the discomfort of stuffiness due to head colds. Sutol was a new treatment formulated with an all-mutton base. Georgian Pharmaceutical Company guaranteed Sutol would permeate the skin and nasal passages.

B & M Liniment, Caragol, and Dr.

Thacher's Magic Rub offered relief from muscle aches, pains, stiffness, bruises, and minor strains. Booth's Healing Balm was ideal for chapped lips and hands, as well as bruises, burns, chafing, and sunburn. Porter's Pain King Salve could be applied to people or "beasts." This ointment could be administered to livestock for cuts, scratches, collar and saddle gall, bruises, caked udders, and sore teats.

Nyal's Catarrhal Balm included instructions in Spanish, Italian, and Polish. Musterole, Snow White Super Pure Liniment, Nurse Brand Salve, and Vaseline Borated Petroleum Jelly were indispensable general household ointments.

Analgesic Balm, Rexall Drug Co, Los Angeles, Boston, St. Louis, USA, "an effective analgesic and counter-irritant that helps relieve discomfort of minor bronchial irritations due to colds, muscular aches and pains due to overexertion, simple headaches, neuralgia and irritation caused by bites of non-poisonous insects," 1-oz, 4″ × 1⅜″ white and blue tube with white plastic lid in 4¼″ × 1⅛″ × 1⅛″ blue and white cardboard box with blue letters, full tube **5.50**

B & M Liniment, mfr since 1913 by F. E. Rollins Co, Boston, MA, "for treatment of muscular aches, pains and stiffness due to overwork, exercise, minor strains, and sprains and bruises where skin remains intact," 8-fl oz, 6¾″ × 2¾″ × 1⅛″ clear glass bottle with black metal lid, yellow label with black letters, ¼-full bottle **8.50**

Balsam of Myrrh, G. C. Hanford Mfg Co, Syracuse, NY, "first aid in the home for minor cuts, burns, bruises, abrasions, sunburn, scalds, chafing, chapped skin, oak and ivy poisoning, insect and mosquito bites, athlete's foot, a liniment for soreness from over-exertion, chilblains, strains," 3-fl oz, 4½″ × 2″ × 1″ clear glass bottle with black plastic lid in 5¼″ × 2¼″ × 1¼″ yellow and blue cardboard box

Bear's Jack Frost, Reg. U.S. Pat. Off., Bear Mfg Co, Winfield, KS, "temporary relief from colds, coughs, and throat irritations when used with massage in vapor for chapped hands and lips," 1-oz, 1⅝" × 1½" clear glass jar with white metal lid, light blue and dark blue label with dark blue and red letters, picture of polar bear, empty jar **5.50**

Bo-Y-Ol' Salve, The Pfeiffer Co, St. Louis, MO, "for minor irritations of the skin," 1-oz, 4¾" × 1¼" silver tube with white plastic lid in 4¾" × 1¼" × 1" gold, white, and blue cardboard box with gold and blue letters, full tube **6.00**

with white and blue letters, instruction sheet, empty bottle **17.00**

1¼-fl oz, 3¾" × 1½" × ¾" clear glass bottle with black plastic lid in 4¼" × 1⅞" × 1⅛" yellow and blue cardboard box with white and blue letters, empty bottle **14.00**

Begy's True Mustarine, S. C. Wells & Co, LeRoy, NY, "for use in place of a mustard plaster or wherever a hot application is indicated as a counter-irritant," 1½-oz, 2⅜" × 1⅝" × 1⅝" yellow and black cardboard box with white and black letters, full unopened box **4.50**

Bleher Concentrated Liniment, mfr by Bleher-Marmon Mfg Co, Lima, OH, "for

any ache or pain with an unbroken surface," 2" × 2" cloudy white glass jar with silver metal lid, brown and black label with red and brown letters, full jar **8.00**

Boil-Ease Drawing Salve, Commerce Drug Co Inc, New York City, "an ideal anesthetic pain-relieving ointment particularly suitable as an application to boils," 1-oz, 1⅞" × 1⅜" brown glass jar with black metal lid, white and red label with black and red letters, formerly Boylene, almost empty **3.00**

Booth's Balm, A Healing Ointment, distr solely by Booth's Hyomei-Co, Ithaca, NY; Fort Erie, ONT, "for chapped lips and hands, burns, bruises, cuts, sunburn, chafing, and skin abrasions," ¾″ × 2⅛″ silver metal container in 2½″ × 2½″ × 1″ white cardboard box with red and blue letters, full container **8.00**

Cadum Ointment, made by The Omega Chemical Co, New York, "for such skin diseases as usually yield to external treatment," 1¼-oz, ¾″ × 2⅛″ beige and brown metal container with beige and brown letters, new-style label adopted May 30, 1918, full container **6.00**

Caragol, Caragol Laboratories, Inc, Cleveland, OH, "for the relief of discomfort associated with muscular strains, simple neuralgia, mosquito and insect bites, tired aching feet, muscular aches and pain due to fatigue and exertion," 4-fl oz, 4¾″ × 1½″ pink and brown plastic bottle with brown letters, **6.25**

Catarrhal Balm, Nyal Co distr, Detroit, USA, "for the relief of catarrh, colds, stuffy head and distress of hay fever," ⅜-oz, 3½″ × ⅞″ yellow tube with silver metal lid in 4¼″ × 1¼″ × ¾″ orange cardboard box with black letters, instruction sheet, translations in Spanish, Polish, and Italian, full tube **7.50**

Chestine Ointment, US Pure Drug Laboratories, Cincinnati, OH, "for the treatment of simple chest and throat congestions due to colds," 1-oz, 1⅝″ × 2″ cloudy white glass jar with black plastic lid, yellow label with black letters, full jar **6.50**

Creo-Derma Ointment, The S. E. Massengill Co, Bristol, TN, "of value in relieving the itching or as an aid in removing the crusts associated with eczema, suggested for barber's itch, nettlerash, eruption of poison ivy, to allay the symptoms of pruritus, as a general purpose ointment, as may be determined by the physician," 2-oz, 5¼″ × 1½″ yellow tube with black plastic lid in 5¼″ × 1¼″ × 1¼″ yellow cardboard box, orange label with black letters, full tube **8.50**

Cuticura Ointment, Potter Drug & Chemical Corp, Malden, MA, USA, "for rashes, blackheads, and externally caused pimples, effective for detergent hands, diaper rash, minor burns, chapping etc.,"

1¾-oz, 1¾″ × 2⅝″ orange, white, and black metal container with orange and black letters, almost-full container **2.50**

4½ oz, 1⅞″ × 2⅝″ textured clear glass jar with white metal lid in 3″ × 3″ × 2″ orange and white cardboard box with black and orange letters, full jar **7.00**

DeWitt's Vaporizing Balm, prepared only at the DeWitt Laboratories, E. C. DeWitt & Co Inc, Chicago, New York, "giving out vapor that is soothing to nasal passages," 1½-oz, 2¼″ × 1½″ clear glass jar with yellow metal lid in 2⅝″ × 2¼″ × 2¼″ white card-

*Hamlins Wizard Oil Liniment, mfr by Myers Laboratories Inc, Warren, PA, "an important useful household remedy for soothing counter-irritant relief in muscular aches, pains, stiffness of neck, shoulders, back, sides and limbs when due to overexertion or exposure, eases pain of minor strains, minor frost bites, mild sunburn and non-venomous insect bites and stings, also useful for soothing counter-irritant effects in minor head cold, simple headaches and simple neuralgia," 2-fl oz, 4⅜″ × 1¾″ × ⅞″ clear glass bottle with black metal lid in 5⅜″ × 1⅞″ × ⅞″ orange cardboard box with black letters, picture of man, ½-full bottle **12.00***

Dr. Lemke's Golden Liniment, prepared by Dr. H. C. Lemke Medicine Co, Chicago, IL, "a counter-irritant for sprains, bruises, congestion of muscles or joints and as an inhibitory antiseptic dressing in minor cuts and wounds," 4-oz, 5½" × 2" × ¾" clear glass jar with gold metal lid in 6¼" × 2½" × 1⅛" brown cardboard box with black letters, est. 1871, picture of man with a horse and woman nursing a sick man, translation in German, instruction sheet, full jar **20.00**

board box with green and orange letters, picture of sunrise over mountains, full jar **7.50**

DeWitt's Witch Hazel Salve (Carbolized), prepared only at The DeWitt Laboratories, E. C. DeWitt & Co Inc, Chicago, IL, "for minor burns, cuts, and abrasions," 1⅛-oz, 4½" × 1½" yellow and green tube with black plastic lid in 5" × 1¼" × 1" yellow, green, and orange cardboard box with black and yellow letters, instruction sheet, full tube **6.00**

Draw-Zit, Hance Bros & White Co, Pharmaceutical Chemists, Philadelphia, PA, "drawing salve," 1-oz, 4½" × 1⅜" white, gray, and orange tube with black plastic lid in 4½" × 1" × 1¼" gray, white, and orange cardboard box with white letters, Spanish translation, full tube **8.75**

Dr. Thacher's Magic Rub, Allied Drug Products Co, Chattanooga, TN, "for quick relief of minor muscular discomforts due to common colds, for simple neuralgia, simple headache, insect bites and stings, sore muscles from fatigue and exertion," 2-oz, 2" × 2" clear glass jar with white metal lid in 2½" × 2¼" × 2¼" red and white cardboard box with blue letters, instruction sheet, full jar **5.50**

Drew's Vaporizing Croup & Pneumonia Salve, The B. H. Drew Chem. Co, Macon, GA, "recommended for colds, croup, pneumonia," 1½-oz, 2½" × 1⅝" clear glass bottle with gold metal lid in 2¾" × 2¼" × 2¼" brown, red, and green cardboard box with green, red, and brown letters **6.25**

Exone, prepared by Duncan Laboratories, St. Louis, MO, "antiseptic dressing and liniment, for cuts, burns, bruises, sunburn, poison ivy, sore muscles, sprains," 4-fl oz, 5⅜" × 2" × 1⅛" clear glass bottle with black metal lid in 6″ × 2⅜″ × 1¼″ red and black cardboard box with white and black letters, full bottle **8.25**

Forni's Heil-oel Liniment, Dr. Peter Fahrney & Sons Co, "has proved effective for over 50 years in the treatment of rheumatic and neuralgic pains, stiff, sore muscles, sprains, bruises, muscular backache, headache, bumps, minor cuts and wounds, sunburn, insect bites, itching or burning feet," 3½-fl oz, 5½″ × 1½″ × 1¾″ clear glass bottle with green metal lid with safety seal in 5¾″ × 1¾″ × 1¾″ brown cardboard box with black letters, instruction sheet, German translation, ¼-full bottle **9.00**

Gold Medal Pink Ointment, S. Pfeiffer Mfg Co, St. Louis, MO, "an effective application for destroying head lice, body lice and crab lice, destroys the nits as well as the vermin," ¾-oz, 3¾″ × 1″ silver tube with white plastic lid in 4½″ × 1⅝″ × ⅞″ red and white box with black letters, instruction sheet, Spanish translation, full tube **5.00**

Gray's Improved Genuine Ointment, mfr by W. F. Gray & Co, Nashville, TN, "aids in relieving the pain and discomfort of minor skin irritations and abrasions, superficial cuts, burns, and minor bruises," ½-oz, ⅝″ × 1½″ gray metal container in 1½″ × 1½″ × ¾″ black and white cardboard box with black letters, full container **7.00**

Hydrosal Ointment, Hydrosal Co, Cincinnati, OH, "a soothing astringent dressing for minor burns, chafing, itching of eczema, minor scalds, minor sunburn, poison ivy, non-poisonous insect stings, rectal itching and irritation, relieves itching and burning of minor skin irritations, of particular value for the tender skin of infants and children," ½-oz, 4″ × ⅝″ light blue and dark blue tube with black plastic lid in 4¼″ × 1⅛″ × ⅝″ light blue and dark blue box with blue and white letters, instruction sheet, full tube **3.00**

Kaiser's World Wonder Salve, prepared by Louise Kaiser, Cedar Grove, IN, "time-tested antiseptic dressing for boils, bruises, cuts, bee stings, frost bites, poison ivy,

Lucky Tiger Ointment, Lucky Tiger Mfg Co, Kansas City, MO, "made to allay itching and burning feet, insect bites, stings, ringworm, itchy scalp irritations, fire and sunburns, externally caused pimples, simple hemorrhoids and rectal irritations all when not caused by systemic conditions," ¾-oz, 1¾″ × 1½″ clear glass jar with black metal lid, yellow, black, and orange label with black and white letters, full jar **10.00**

new sores, old sores, and wounds, first aid in burns, nothing better for carbuncles," 1¾″ × 2¼″ cloudy white jar with blue metal lid, orange label with black letters, full jar **7.00**

Manzaid Muscle and Chest Rub, Manzaid Drug Co, Oberlin, OH, "a counter-irritant serviceable in neuralgia, pain in joints, articular rheumatism, inflamed glands and all forms of stiffness, symptoms of deep-seated inflammation and other conditions where a counter-irritant is indicated," 1¼-oz, 2⅛″ × 1¼″ green glass jar with white metal lid, white label with green letters, full jar **4.25**

Menthoin, Rigo Mfg Co, Nashville, TN, "a soothing application for the relief of discomforts due to colds," 1½-fl oz, 2½″ × 1½″ clear glass jar with black metal lid, red and orange label with black letters, full jar **6.00**

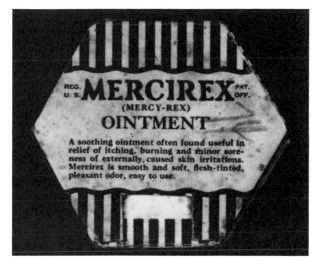

Mercirex Ointment, made in USA for The Mercirex Co, Milford, DE, USA, printed in USA, "a soothing ointment often found useful in relief of itching, burning and minor soreness of externally caused skin irritations," 1-oz, 1⅝" × 2" hexagonal cloudy white glass jar with yellow and brown lid in 1⅞" × 2⅛" brown-and-white striped box with brown letters, picture of a woman on lid of jar, full jar 12.00

Mentholatum, The Mentholatum Co, Buffalo, NY; Wichita, KS; Bridgeburg, ONT; London, ENG, "a soothing external application for head colds, chapped skin, sunburn, nasal irritation, simple headaches," 2½" × 2⅛" cloudy white glass jar with brown metal lid, brown label with black letters, full jar **12.00**

Merrell's Penetrating Oil Liniment, J. S. Merrell Drug Co, St. Louis, MO, "for sore, stiff and cramped muscles, minor sprains and strains, bruises, insect bites, relieves simple neuralgia and stiff neck to exposure and drafts," 1½"-fl oz, 4⅜" × 1⅝" × ½" clear glass bottle with red metal lid in 5" × 1⅞" × ⅞" yellow cardboard box with black and red letters, instruction sheet, full bottle **10.00**

Moruquent Ointment, The S. E. Massengill Co, Bristol, TN, "for dry skin, chafing, winter eczema, abrasions, diaper rash, sunburn, minor burns, minor cuts and abrasion, routine nipple care," 1-oz, 5" × 1¼" white tube with black plastic lid in 5⅛" × 1⅛" × 1⅛" gray and white cardboard box with maroon, gray, and white letters, instruction sheet, full tube **8.00**

Musterole, The Musterole Co, Cleveland, OH, "for the distress of local congestion, muscular soreness and coughs caused by chest colds, minor throat irritations, muscular aches and pains, sprains, simple

headache and neuralgia, frosted feet and unbroken chilblains," ⅞-oz, 3¾" × 1¼" white and black tube with black plastic lid, white and black letters, almost-empty tube **3.00**

Mutton Tallow with Camphor, prepared only by the Roosa & Ratliff Chemical Co, Cincinnati, OH, "for minor cuts, chapped hands, rough skin," ⅜-oz, ¾" × 1¾" × 2¾" yellow metal container with black letters, picture of a sheep, free sample, full container **12.00**

Nurse Brand Salve, The DePree Co, Holland, MI, "a soothing ointment for family use, valuable in relieving superficial burns, surface wounds and minor irritation of the rectum," 1-oz, 4¼" × 1" white tube with black plastic lid in 4¾" × 1⅜" × 1" blue, black, yellow, and white box with white and black letters, picture of nurse, full tube **10.00**

Omega Rub, Omega Chemical Co Inc, Jersey City, NJ, "for relief of muscular aches and pains, discomfort of colds, headache, neuralgia and rheumatic pains," 1-oz, 3½" × 1" green and white tube with black plastic lid in 4¼" × 1¼" × 1¼" green and white cardboard box with white and green letters, instruction sheet **8.50**

Palmer's Skin Success Ointment, E. T. Brown Drug Co Inc, East Newark, Har-

Mother's Salve, mfr only by The Mother's Remedies Co, Chicago, IL, "soothes, relieves nasal congestion in common colds and promotes healing of burns, bruises, etc.," ½-oz, 1¼″ × 1½″ cloudy white glass jar with white metal lid in 1⅝″ × 1⅜″ × 1⅝″ white cardboard box with black letters, picture of women, instruction sheet, full jar 10.00

rison, NJ, USA, "for temporary relief of itching and scaling due to psoriasis," .50-oz, ½″ × 1½″ red metal container in 2″ × 2½″ × ¾″ red and white cardboard box with black letters, instruction sheet, full container **6.50**

Pike's Green Mountain Salve, Est. by C. C. Pike in 1883, mfr by Pike Mfg Co, Binghamton, NY, "for sale by leading druggists, for burns, bites, stings, corns, sores, infections, bruises, boils," 3¾″ × ¾″ green paper roll with black letters, picture of pines, full roll **6.00**

Porter's Pain King Salve, The Geo. H. Rundle Co, Piqua, OH, "for cuts, bruises, sores, wounds, burns, boils, piles, felons, lumbago, chapped and cracked skin, also to relieve cold on the chest and spasmodic croup, for stock cuts, scratches, collar and saddle galls, bruises, sore teats on cows, caked udder," 3½-oz, 1″ × 3¼″ blue and white metal container with blue letters, empty container **12.00**

Radway's Ready Relief (RRR), owned and distr since 1847 by Radwayola, New York, NY, USA, "externally as a counter-irritant liniment, internally as a carminative," 1⅞-fl oz, 6″ × 2″ × 1″ brown box with black letters, picture of an angel with a jar of RRR and two people, cellophane-sealed box **18.00**

Ramon's Rub, Brown Mfg Co, LeRoy, NY, "to help relieve superficial congestion accompanying common colds," 1½-oz, 2¼″ × 1¾″ clear blue glass jar with metal lid, yellow and blue label with blue and white letters, picture of "The Little Doctor," full jar **8.75**

Richard's Menthol Cream, A. B. Richards Medicine Co, Chattanooga, TN, "gives relief to minor throat irritations and nasal irritations, congestion and excessive secretion caused by or associated with head colds, is an aid in relieving itching due to minor skin irritation and is a soothing dressing for chapped hands or minor burns," 1½-oz, 2¼″ × 1½″ clear glass jar with blue plastic lid in 2¾″ × 1⅞″ × 1¾″ white cardboard box with orange and black letters, pictures of men and women using the cream **6.00**

Roche's Embrocation, W Edwards & Sons, Proprietors 11, Springfield, London E. S., prepared in New York, and distr by E. Fougera & Co Inc, New York, NY, "for external use only," 2-fl oz, 3¾″ × 1¼″ brown glass bottle with brown metal lid, brown label with black letters, picture of unicorn, lion, and a crown, signature of Roche, brown-paper-wrapped bottle **10.00**

Rowles Mentho-Sulphur, Phenol-Camphor Compound, reg. U.S. Whitehall Pat. Off.,

Pixine, The Pixine Co, Troy, NY, "a healing antiseptic ointment for burns, boils, infected wounds, ulcers, cuts, colds, pneumonia, and skin diseases, an ideal surgical dressing for inflammations, congestion and tissue building," 5″ × 1½″ blue and white tube with black plastic lid in 5″ × 1½″ × 1″ blue and white box with white letters, instruction sheet, full tube **6.25**

Whitehall Pharmacol Co, New York, NY, "for the relief of itching of the skin due to non-poisonous insect bites and chafing, also for relief of itching of scalp and removal of scales of dandruff, relieves temporarily the itching of hemorrhoids," 1⅛-oz, 2¼″ × 1⅝″ glass bottle in 2⅜″ × 1¾″ × 1¾″ yellow cardboard box with black letters, picture of girl, full bottle **8.75**

Rumarub, S. Pfeiffer Mfg Co, St. Louis, MO, "external analgesic application to aid in the relief of aches and pains associated with rheumatism, muscular lumbago, minor strains and sprains, muscular aches, pains, lameness and soreness due to over-exertion, simple neuralgia, exposure, dampness and fatigue," 5-fl oz, 6¼″ × 2½″ × 1″ clear glass bottle with white plastic safety-sealed lid in 7″ × 3″ × 1¾″ red and white box with blue, red, and white letters, full bottle **8.50**

Runion's White Wonder Salve, White Wonder Chemical Co, Montgomery, AL, "for simple neuralgia and headaches, when caused by head colds, for the discomforts of nasal congestion due to colds," ⅝-oz, 2⅛″ × 1⅜″ cloudy white glass jar with black plastic lid in 2¼″ × 2¾″ × 2¾″ white and blue cardboard box with blue and white letters, instruction sheet, full jar **7.00**

Sayman Liniment, mfr by Sayman Products Co, St. Louis, MO, "an effective rubefacient application for relief of the discomfort of muscular aches, soreness and pains caused by fatigue or over-exertion," 3-fl oz, 5¼″ × 1⅞″ clear glass bottle with white metal lid in 5½″ × 2″ × 1″ yellow, white, and blue box with blue letters, picture of man, instructions, full bottle **11.00**

Sisson's Household Ointment, Philip Sisson, Canadaigua, NY, "it is very soothing to all kinds of wounds and will not blister, it is helpful for cuts, burns, salt rheum, barber's itch, chafing, bites and stings of insects, hemorrhoids or piles, chapped hands or face etc.," 2½″ × 1⅞″ cloudy white glass jar with black plastic lid, white label with black letters, "none genuine without this signature: Philip Sisson," full jar **5.00**

Snow White Super-Pure Liniment, American Co Distr, Memphis, TN, "an ideal all-purpose household liniment for muscular soreness, aches, simple sprains and pains due to exposure and fatigue," 4-fl oz, 6½″ × 2⅓″ × ⅞″ clear glass bottle with black plastic lid, white and orange label with gray and white letters, ½-full bottle **3.50**

Sutol, guaranteed and distr by Georgian Pharmacal Co, Atlanta, GA, "for local congestion and irritation accompanying head colds, chest colds," 1-oz, 2¼″ × 1½″ blue glass jar with white metal lid in 2¾″ × 2″ × 2″ yellow and blue cardboard box with blue and white letters, instruction sheet, picture of sheep, full jar **7.50**

Thunder Cloud Brand Famous Liniment, prepared for Chief Thunder Cloud, Cincinnati, OH, "an excellent household liniment

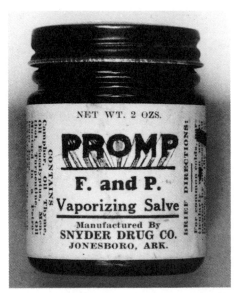

Promp, mfr by Snyder Drug Co, Jonesboro, AR, "for common colds, particularly when accompanied by soreness and tightness in the upper part of the chest or throat," 1½-oz, 2½" × 1¾" clear blue jar with black metal lid, white label with black letters, full jar **6.00**

to relieve minor muscular aches and pains due to fatigue, sprains, bruises, frostbite, insect bites and simple headache and neuralgia," 1-fl oz clear glass jar in 4¾" × 1⅛" × 1⅛" white cardboard box with blue letters, picture of an Indian man, empty jar **2.00**

Vaseline Borated Petroleum Jelly, the descriptive name of this product is "Borated Petroleum Jelly Vaseline," a registered trademark of Chesebrough Pond's Inc, New York, NY, made in USA, "a soothing dressing for minor skin irritations, irritations of the nostrils due to head colds, chafing in babies and adults, minor burns," ⅗-oz, 4" × 1" green and white tube with white plastic lid in 4⅜" × 1" × 1" green and white cardboard box with black letters, full tube **6.25**

Vicks Vapo-Rub, prepared by Vicks Chemical Co, Greensboro, NC, USA, "an external treatment for certain forms of local conges-

tion and irritation," 1½-fl oz, 2⅜" × 1½" brown glass jar with red metal lid, blue and white label with red and blue letters, full jar **8.00**

Woolley's Ointment, prepared for John W. Woolley Remedy Co, Wabash, IN, USA, "useful for relief of muscular soreness due to exercise or exposure, and for massaging the chest and throat to provide warming effects," 1-oz, 2⅛" × 1⅜" clear green glass jar with black plastic lid, white label with blue letters, full jar **8.50**

Stomach Products

Gastric distress was almost as prevalent a malady as irregularity. If a given medication did not produce the desired results, one could try numerous other products on the shelves. The term "upset stomach" encompassed heartburn, acid stomach, gas distress, bloating, nervous stomach, indigestion, sour eructations, gastric hyperacidity, and unpleasant breath. Although sleeplessness and sick headache due to acid indigestion appeared far-fetched, one company guaranteed relief from these maladies as well.

Liquid Sedagel soothed and coated the stomach and intestines with a fine protective coating. Trialka with belladonna absorbed hyperacidity as rapidly as a sponge. If an individual's digestion was retarded, taking Winthrop's product might sweeten the stomach.

It was not uncommon for companies to offer free samples of products to potential customers. The E. C. DeWitt & Co. Inc. of Chicago, for example, offered DeWitt's Antacid Powder in a small blue, black, and white box. This product later became available in an assortment of larger sizes.

Tablets were the most popular way to take antacids. Requa's Charcola Tablets were simple and effective. According to a package date 1961, this product had been on the market for many years. A 1937 bottle of Adla Tablets sold for $1. The bottle contained sixty-three tablets, a full three-week treatment.

See also Diarrhea Remedies, Infant and Children Laxatives, and Laxatives.

STOMACH LIQUIDS

Gastron, Winthrop Laboratories, Div of Sterling Drug Inc, New York, NY, "for the treatment of retarded digestion associated with a deficiency of gastric secretions," 6-fl oz, 5¾" × 2½" × 1⅜" clear glass bottle with black plastic lid in 6" × 2½" × 1¾" green and white cardboard box with green letters, full bottle **6.00**

Lightning Hot Drops, mfr by The Herb Medicine Co, Dayton, OH, "for gastric discomfort caused by gas in the stomach," 2-fl oz, 3¾" × 1¾" × 1" clear glass bottle with

black lid, blue and white label with blue letters, almost-full bottle **6.00**

1½-fl oz, 4⅜" × 1¾" × ½" clear glass bottle with black metal lid, tan label with blue letters, empty bottle **3.50**

Trialka, Commerce Drug Co Inc, Div Del Laboratories, Inc, Formingdale, Long Island, NY, "for stomach upsets and nervous stomachs," 14-fl oz, 6" × 2¾" × 1¾" white plastic bottle with white plastic lid in 6¼" × 3" × 2" blue and white cardboard box with black and blue letters, full bottle **10.00**

STOMACH POWDERS

Acidine, Consolidated Royal Chemical Corp, Chicago, IL, "for the relief of sour and acid stomach due to stomach hyperacidity, acid eructations and heartburn," 7 packets, 3¾" × 2⅜" × ¾" yellow and green cardboard box with green letters, full box **7.00**

Milk of Trinesium, Abbot Laboratories, North Chicago, IL, antacid, 12-fl oz, 7" × 3" × 2¼" blue glass bottle with green, black, and white label and black and white letters, ½-full bottle 13.00

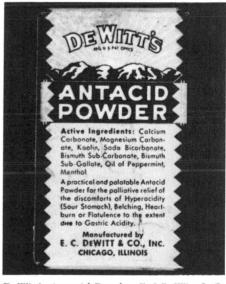

DeWitt's Antacid Powder, E C DeWitt & Co Inc, Chicago, IL, "quick palliative relief of indigestion, heartburn, sour stomach caused by gastric hyperacidity," 4-oz, 4" × 2⅛" × 2⅛" blue and black cardboard box with blue cardboard pop-out lid, black and white letters, picture of sunrise over mountains, full box 4.75

Blake Soda Bicarbonate, distr by Blake Pharmacal Co, Allegan, MI, 1-lb, 5½" × 2½" metal cylinder with white metal lid, black and white letters, full cylinder **8.00**

4-oz, 2½" × 1⅞" metal cylinder with metal pop-out lid, orange and black label with black and white letters, full cylinder **5.00**

Carbamine, Consumer Products Division, Key Pharmaceuticals, Inc, Miami, FL, "quick relief of acid indigestion, soothes and promotes healing of irritated membranes," 12 packets, 2½" × 5" × 1¼" pink and white cardboard box with black letters, full box **7.25**

Carbonate of Magnesia, mfr for McKesson & Robbins, Inc, by Henry K. Davies & Co Inc, New York, NY, 1-oz, 2¾" × 2⅛" × ¾" blue cardboard box with white letters, full box **4.50**

GE-7 Carbonates Compound, United Drug Co, Boston, St. Louis, USA, "alkalizer, a

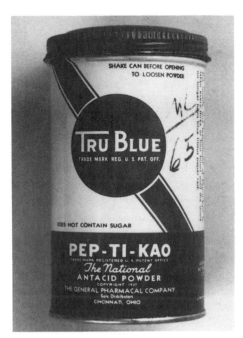

Pep-Ti-Kao, The National Antacid Powder, The General Pharmacal Co, Sole Distr, Cincinnati, OH, "assist in dispelling gas," 1-oz, 4¼" × 2½" pink, blue, and maroon metal can with maroon metal lid and maroon and white letters, copyright 1937, full can 8.50

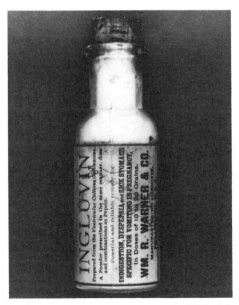

Ingluvin, Wm. R. Warner & Co, Philadelphia, PA, USA, "for indigestion, dyspepsia and sick stomach, specific for vomiting in pregnancy," 1-oz, 4" × 1½" round, clear glass, cork-stoppered bottle, tan and black label with black letters, genuine Wm. R. Warner signature across face of label in red letters, full bottle 51.00

palatable antacid," 5-oz, 5⅞" × 2¼" × 2¼" clear glass bottle with white metal lid, brown and tan label with brown and tan letters, full bottle **11.00**

Pulvis Alkantis, Distr by Lafayette Pharmacal, Lafayette, IN, USA, "antacid alkalizer," 1-oz, 3⅜" × 2" × 2" cardboard box with white and yellow label and black letters, full box **6.75**

STOMACH TABLETS

Adla Tablets, one of the Adler-I-Ka quality products distr by the Adlerika Co, St. Paul, MN, "useful in acidity, sour stomach, indigestion, heartburn, bloating, belching and other conditions due to hyperacidity of the stomach," 63 tabs, 5¼" × 2¼" × 1⅜" green glass bottle with white metal lid, beige label with green letters, picture of

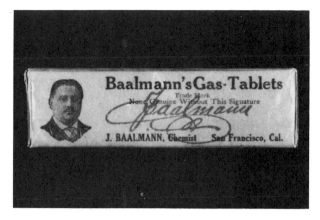

man's head, copyright 1933, almost-full bottle **8.50**

Antacid Tablets, Nyal Co distr. Detroit, MI, USA, "for relief of the discomforts resulting from excessive gastric acidity," 100 tabs, 4¼″ × 1¾″ × 1⅛″ clear brown bottle with white metal lid, green and brown label with brown letters, full bottle **5.00**

"A" Plus, distr by Vick Chemical Co, div of Richardson-Merrell Inc., New York, NY, "A" Plus is a trademark, Reg US Pat. Off., "relieves indigestion distress as no plain antacid can," 10 tabs in 2¼″ × ½″ white and gold foil roll with red and blue letters, full unopened roll **2.75**

"Caroid" & Soda Bicarb. Tablets, The American Ferment Co, Buffalo, NY, "invaluable in dyspepsia and indigestion" 45 tabs, 3″ × 1¼″ × ½″ clear brown glass bottle with cork stopper in 3″ × 1½″ × ¾″ gray cardboard box with red and blue letters, instruction sheet, full bottle **18.00**

Dia-Bisma Antacid Tablets, The Penslar Co, Inc, New York, NY, "a pleasant tasting alkaline preparation for the relief of discomfort due to excessive gastric acidity," 30 tabs, 2¼″ × 2¾″ × ¼″ green and brown cardboard box with white letters, full box **7.50**

Dill's Digesters, mfr by the Dill Co, Norristown, PA, "for symptoms of excessive stomach acidity," 40 tabs, 2½″ × ⅞″ × ⅞″ clear glass bottle with red metal lid in yellow and red box with black letters, new carton adopted 1935, full bottle **4.50**

Gelusil, Arner-chilcott, Laboratories Div, Morris Plains, NJ, "for when heartburn makes you miserable," 12 tabs, 3″ × 2½″ × ½″ white cardboard box with red letters, full plastic wrapped in pairs box **3.75**

Nulacin, made in England by Horlicks Limited, Pharmaceutical div, Slough Bucks distr, Consolidated Royal Chemical Corp, Chicago, IL, "indicated for the relief of gastric hyperacidity," 25 tabs, 5½″ × 1″ metal cylinder with silver metal lid, blue and beige label with blue and beige letters, full cylinder **8.00**

Pape's Dia-pape-Sen Compound, Sterling Products Inc, distr, successor to Pape, Thompson, & Pape Co, Wheeling WV, "for stomach distress, loss of appetite, sour stomach, belching of gas caused by acidity," 43 tabs, 3⅝″ × 1⅝″ cardboard cylinder, green and white label with brown and white letters, full unopened cylinder **12.00**

Pfunder's Tablets, distr by Grove Laboratories Inc, St. Louis, MO, "for hyperacid stomach," 102 tabs, 5¾″ × 3⅝″ × 2½″ yellow and green cardboard box with brown letters, picture of man's face, full box, plastic sealed in packages of six **12.00**

Riopan, Ayerst Laboratories Inc, New York, NY, "fast and prolonged relief from gastric hyperacidity," 60 tabs, 2½″ × 6¼″ × 1⅛″ white and green cardboard box with red letters, full plastic-sealed box **4.00**

Tracy Tablets, The Tracy Co Inc, distr reg. U.S. Pat. Off., Hartford, CT, "for the tempo-

Bell-Ans made only by Bells Co Inc, mfg Chemists, Orangeburg, NY, USA, "for indigestion due to excess acid," 100 tabs, 2⅞" × 1⅞" × 1" clear brown glass bottle with black metal lid in 3' × 2" × 1" yellow cardboard box with red and green letters, full unopened bottle **7.50 (older)**

Bell-Ans, made only by Bells Co Inc, mfg Chemists, Orangeburg, NY, USA, "for indigestion due to excess acid," 30 tabs, 2¾" × ¾" clear brown glass bottle with black metal lid in 3" × 1" × 1" yellow and red cardboard box, instruction sheet, full unopened bottle **5.75**

Requa's Charcoal Tablets, Requa Mfg Co Inc, Brooklyn, NY, USA, "for relief in gas and acid stomach," 70 tabs, 3½ × 1⅞" metal can with pop-out lid, black and white label with black and white letters (center) **6.50**
100 tabs, 3" × 2½" metal can with pop-out lid, black, blue, and white label with black and white letters (left) **8.00**
150 tabs, 4" × 2½" metal can with pop-out lid, black and white label with black and white letters (right) **9.50**

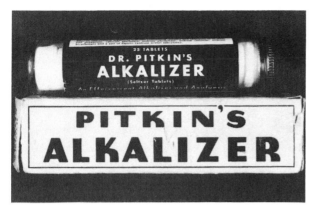

Pitkin's Alkalizer, Inland Laboratories Inc, Indianapolis, IN, "a pleasant and effective aid in relieving headache, gas on stomach, sour stomach, and heartburn when caused by an excess of acid in the digestive system," 25 tabs, 5⅞" × 1¼" clear glass bottle with blue metal lid in 6½" × 1⅝" × 1⅝" blue and white cardboard box with blue letters, full unopened bottle **10.00**

rary relief of indigestion, gas, heartburn, sour stomach," 75 tabs, 4" × 1¾" × 1⅛" clear brown glass bottle with black metal lid, beige label with black letters, full unopened bottle **7.00**

Trulase, Smith, Miller & Patch Inc, New York, NY, "for relief of digestive discomfort," 100 tabs, 3⅜" × 1⅞" clear brown glass bottle with yellow metal lid, maroon and yellow label with maroon letters, full unopened bottle **5.75**

Tums Carminative, Antacid, Lewis-Howe Co, made in USA, St. Louis, MO, USA; Canadian Laboratory, Windsor, Ontario, CAN, "for the relief of hyperacidity, acid indigestion, sour stomach, gas, heartburn, and conditions where an antacid is indicated," 3-roll, 1¾" × 2" × ½" package, blue label with white letters, full unopened cellophane wrapped package **8.00**

UDGA Tablets, Compounded for and packed by UDGA, Inc, St. Paul, MN, "intended for the temporary relief from distress after eating caused by excess stomach acidity, sour stomach, heartburn," 20 tabs, 3¼" × 2¾" × ⅜" white, gray, blue, and green box with blue letters, full unopened cellophane-wrapped box **5.00**

Suntan Products

Including suntan products here is important from a historical perspective. With the advent of the classic one-piece maillot bathing suit and the itsy-bitsy-teenie-weenie-yellow-polka-dot bikini, modesty was replaced with concern for a smooth, even tan.

The first commercial suntan product was Pada, which had been issued to American flyers in the Pacific during World War II.

Tanfastic IR-9 promoted a natural tan and offered burn protection. Its creamy white lotion would not stain clothing. As an added bonus, this product included an insect repellant. The convenient yellow plastic bottle was easy to spot on the beach, and there was no worry about broken glass.

Panama Jack and his "crew," which provided varying degrees of skin protection, was approximately thirty years away.

Kantan Suntan Lotion, The Norwich Pharmaceutic Co, Norwich, NY, 3-fl oz bottle, orange rubber-like coating on bottle with white letters, full bottle **4.00**

Tanfastic IR-9 Suntan Lotion, Sea & Ski Royyey Co, Reno, NV, "lotion with insect repellent," 7" × 6½" × 9" tan and red box with red and black letters, bee figure, display box only **7.50**

4-oz plastic bottle in 2⅜" × 5⅝" × 1¼" blue, white, yellow, and red box, picture of insect, lady in bathing suit, man in fishing gear holding fishing rod, full bottle **8.50**

2-oz plastic tube in 1⅞″ × 1⅛″ × 5⅝″ blue, white, yellow, and red box, picture of insect, lady in bathing suit, man in fishing gear holding fishing rod, full tube **6.00**

Tannic Spray, Gebauer Chemical Co, Cleveland, OH, "spray for burns, cuts, bites, poison ivy," round brown bottle with plastic and metal spray top in 1⅞″ × ⅝″ × 1⅞″ yellow, turquoise, tan, white, and black box, woman in bathing suit, water behind her, ½-full bottle **6.50**

Tartan, McKesson & Robbins Inc, New York, NY; Bridgeport, CT, "suntan lotion," 4-fl oz clear glass bottle with red, black, and white (tartan plaid) label with black and red letters, full bottle **4.50**

for cuts, burns, insect bites, loose dandruff, and after shaving.

Glycenol, The Meier Dental & Surgical Mfg Co, Berlin, London, St. Louis, "mouth, nose, throat, or general antiseptic use," 4-oz clear round glass bottle with cork stopper, tan and black label with black letters, name embossed on bottle, almost-full bottle **16.00**

Listerine, Lambert Pharmacal Co, St. Louis, MO, "antiseptic mouthwash," 3-fl oz, 4¼″ × 1½″ clear glass bottle, embossed name and company on bottle, company initials on lid, ½-full bottle **15.00**

Pain-A-Lay, The Glessner Co, Findlay, OH, "mouth and throat antiseptic," 16-fl oz, 6½″ × 2¾″ round brown bottle with pink,

Throat Products

With the advent of specialized throat products, there was one less use for the old standby remedy—a gargle of warm saltwater.

MOUTHWASHES

M. S. Severa's Antisepsol was a wholesome, refreshing, and soothing product for minor throat irritations. The alcohol content was 25 percent, and the active ingredients included benzoic acid, thymol, oil red, thyme, menthol, methyl salicylate, eucalyptol, and boric acid.

Ten drops of Garglette and a pinch of salt were added to a glass of lukewarm water. According to the instructions on the Garglette bottle, this mixture was "snuffled" up the nose or as a nasal douche or spray once or twice a day.

Mouthwashes could also be used

Garglette, The Garglette Co, Indianapolis, IN, antiseptic for mouth, nose, throat, and skin irritations, 12-oz round clear glass bottle with black, yellow, and white label with black and white letters **10.00**

black, and white label and black and white letters, full bottle **8.00**

Pepsodent Antiseptic, Pepsodent Div, Lever Bros Co, Chicago, IL, "mouth wash, gargle, and external antiseptic," 1⅛-fl oz clear glass bottle in 1¾″ × 3¾″ × 1¾″ white, pink horizontal stripes, and navy box with white and navy letters, almost-full bottle **5.00**

7-oz, 5¾″ × 2¼″ clear round glass bottle with light blue and white label and letters, empty bottle **2.25**

Reef, Warner-Lambert Pharm. Co, Morris Plains, NJ, "antiseptic mouth wash and sore throat gargle," 7-fl oz clear glass bottle with navy, green, white, and pea green label and letters, almost-full bottle **4.75**

1-pt, 6-fl oz clear glass bottle, full bottle **11.00**

Severa's Antisepsol, Myers Laboratories Inc, Warren, PA, "mouthwash, gargle, skin irritations," 8-fl oz round clear glass bottle in 6¼″ × 2⅜″ × 2⅜″ box, white label with black letters, picture of W. F. Severa on front and back, no box lid, full bottle **8.50**

THROAT MEDICINES

Dr. Hobson's Throat Lozenges sold for 15¢ and contained twenty-two lozenges. They were composed of pure and selected ingredients and were prepared under the supervision of a competent pharmacist. Haywood's Lime Flavored Sulphur and Cream Of Tartar Lozenges contained the active therapeutic ingredients cream of tartar and sulphur. The package included a note proclaiming that the beneficial effects of sulphur were well known.

Formamint Tablets were used in place of gargles. In the 1950s "New" Pinex wild-cherry-flavored throat lozenges were introduced. This medication contained an antibiotic, an anesthetic, and an antihistamine.

Lozenges could also be used for coughs, dust inhalation, tickling in the throat, and bronchial irritation due to colds.

Ballard's Golden Oil, Bangor Candy Co, Bangor, ME, "cold, coughs, minor throat discomfort, external use for aches, pains, strains, bruises," 2-oz, 3¾″ × 1½″ clear glass round bottle in tan wrapper with black letters, picture of a two-wheeled horse-drawn buggy, full bottle **15.00**

Dr. Hobson's Throat Lozenges, Pfeiffer Chem. Co, New York, St. Louis, "hoarseness, coughs, throat and bronchial irritation," 2¾″ × 1½″ × ¾″ tan box with black letters, full box **3.00**

Dristets (lozenges), Whitehall Laboratories, Inc, New York, NY, "relief of minor sore throat," ten lozenges, 2¼″ × 1¾″ clear glass round jar, full jar **6.00**

Formamint Tablets, The Bauer Chemical Co, Inc, New York, St. Louis, Toronto, 50 tabs, brown bottle with embossed name on sides with 3⅝″ × 2″ × 1¼″ red, yellow, and white label, full bottle **5.75**

Haywood's Lozenges, Pfeiffer Chemical Co, New York, St. Louis, "lime flavored, sulphur and cream of tartar throat lozenges," 36 lozenges, 3″ × 1¾″ × 1″ tan and orange box with dark blue letters, full box **6.50**

Locane, Wall's Drugs, Indianapolis, IN, "minor sore throat," 12 troches, 2¾″ × ¾″ plastic cylinder, yellow and white label with black letters, full cylinder **5.25**

Micrin Lozenges, Johnson & Johnson, New Brunswick, NJ, "relief of minor sore throat," 18 lozenges, 3¼″ × 2⅛″ × ⅞″ gold, white, and turquoise box with black letters, full box **7.00**

Neo-Aqua-Drin, McKesson & Robbins, Inc, New York, NY; Bridgeport, CT, 12 lozenges, 2⅝″ × ⅝″ plastic cylinder with tan and wine label and wine letters, full cylinder **4.50**

Neohydrin, Lakeside Laboratories, Inc, Milwaukee, WI, 50 tabs, 2¾″ × 1⅛″ × ⅞″ clear glass bottle with metal cap, blue and white label with black and white letters, ¾-full bottle **3.00**

Nyal Bronchials, Nyal Co, Detroit, MI, "for coughs and hoarseness," 30 lozenges, 3⅜" × 1½" × ¾" tan, white, and orange slide-open box with black letters, full box **4.50**

Pinex Wild Cherry Throat Lozenges, Pinex Co Inc, New York, NY, 10 lozenges, 3¾" × 1½" × ⅞" red, white, and blue box with red, white, and blue letters, foil-wrapped lozenges, full box **5.00**

Rexall-Biokets, Rexall Drug Co, Los Angeles, St. Louis, Boston, USA; Toronto, CAN, "for minor throat irritations," 35 troches, brown bottle with metal cap in 3½" × 1⅞" × 1⅜" black box with green and white letters, full bottle **6.00**

Tyzomint, The Blue Line Chemical Co, St. Louis, MO, "for minor throat irritations," 10 lozenges, 2" × ¾" plastic vial, blue and white label with blue and white letters, full vial **3.75**

Tonics, Minerals, and Vitamins

The labels on many tonic bottles stated that the bright red color of the blood needed to be maintained. Hood's Peptiron was an excellent example of the popular early tonics. The active ingredients were pepsin, reduced iron, celery, quinine sulphate, manganese sulphate, extract of gentian, asafetida, podophyllin, capsicum, castile soap, and aloin.

Zestin Fortified Tonic Elixir, Ozomulsion Cod Liver Oil Tonic, and Ostrex Tonic Tablets are considered transitional between tonics and vitamins. Vitawine iron and vitamin tonic was both a tonic and a vitamin product.

Squibb's Rubrafolin, Upjohn's Super D Drops, Knoll Pharmaceutical Company's Vita-Metrazol, and Miller Laboratories' Vitamins A and D could truly be termed "vitamins." And how many individuals who lived in the 1950s could forget Miles Laboratories' One A Day Vitamins?

ABDEC Drops, Parke-Davis & Co, Detroit, MI, 15-cc brown bottle with dropper in 1" × 2" × 3½" tan and wine box, dated February 1969, full bottle **1.00**

A-D Percomorph Liveroil, Abbott Labs, N. Chicago, IL, 100 caps, brown bottle in 1½" × 4" × 1½" green, white, and black box, full bottle **7.00**

Blaud's Pills, McKesson & Robbins Inc, New York, Bridgeport, Montreal, "iron pill since 1833," 100 pills, green bottle with black and gold tin cap, tan and wine label and letters with gold leaves and scales, full bottle **8.00**

Calirad Wafers, The Bayer Co Inc, New York, NY, "calcium, phosphorus and vitamin D compound," 3⅜" × 2⅞" × 1¼" tan, white, red, and brown can with tan, white, red, and brown letters, empty can **12.00**

Cole Iodo-Niacin, Cole Chemical Co, St. Louis, MO, 100 tabs, 1½" × 2¾" round

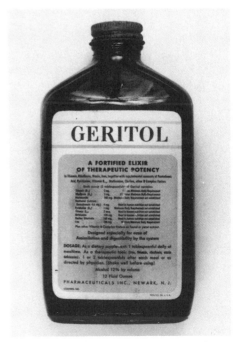

*Geritol, Pharmaceuticals Inc, Newark, NJ, dietary supplement, "Alcohol 12% by volume," 12-fl oz, 6¼" × 3" × 1⅞" clear glass bottle with brown, orange, and white label with brown letters, ¼-full bottle **10.00***

brown bottle with red, white, and blue label, instruction sheet, full bottle **5.50**

Defender Multiple Vitamins, The Globe Laboratories Inc, St. Louis, MO, 48 caps, 1⅝″ × 1¼″ × 3½″ brown bottle, red and white label with flying bald eagle and black and white letters, full bottle **7.75**

Dispadal, E. R. Squibb & Sons, New York, NY, "multiple vitamin drops," 50-cc brown octagonal bottle with dropper in 1¾″ × 2½″ × 3½″ tan and brown box, no lid, full bottle **6.00**

Gude's Pepto-Mangan, M. J. Breitenbach Co, New York, NY, "iron and manganese tonic," 11-oz brown octagonal bottle, name and ounces embossed on one side, in orange, white, and black octagonal box, M. J. Breitenbach signature on bottle and box, full bottle **16.00**

Hemo-Genin, Winthrop-Stearns Inc, New York, NY; Windsor, Ontario, CAN, 100 caps, 2″ × 1¼″ × 4¼″ brown bottle with

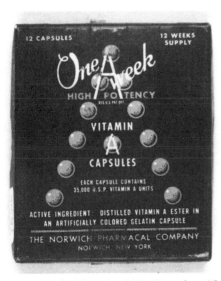

*One-A-Week Vitamin "A" Capsules, The Norwich Pharmacal Co, Norwich, NY, Vitamin "A", "High potency—one capsule a week," "Wartime Container," 12 caps, 3⅛″ × 2⅝″ × ¾″ black and orange cardboard box with orange and white letters, instruction sheet, full box **15.00**

blue and white label and letters, full bottle **5.00**

Kinney Fortified Yeast Tablets, Kinney & Co, Columbus, IN, "vitamin B complex," 100 tabs, 4¼″ × 1⅛″ × 1¾″ brown bottle with yellow, brown, and white label and brown and white letters, full bottle **8.00**

Licuron-B, Lakeside Laboratories, Milwaukee, WI, "each tablet contains daily dose— copper and iron and ⅓ of daily requirement for vitamin B1, B2, and niacinamide," 100 tabs, 1¼″ × 2″ × 4¼″ brown bottle with pale blue, white, and dark blue label with white and dark blue letters, full bottle **4.75**

Metagen, Parke-Davis & Co, Detroit, MI, "vitamin capsules," 50 caps, 4½″ × 1¾″ × 1″ brown corked-stoppered bottle, full bottle **13.00**

Methischol Caps, US Vitamin & Pharm. Corp, Div of Arlington-Funk Labs, New York, NY, 100 caps, round brown bottle with black and white label and letters, full bottle **7.00**

Novo-Basic, E. R. Squibb & Sons, New York, NY, 60 tabs, clear glass bottle, 1⅝″ × 1½″ × 3¼″ pale green and white box with red and brown letters, full bottle **5.75**

Nutrex, Nutrex Co Inc, New York, NY, "a nutritional concentrate 'dried yeast and whole dried liver,' " 84 tabs, brown bottle in 1⅞″ × 1½″ × 3½″ yellow box with dark green and red letters, full bottle **5.50**

Ostrex, Commerce Drug Co Inc, Pektamol Laboratories Inc, New York City, "tonic tablets," 48 tabs, brown round bottle in 1½″ × 1⅝″ × 3″ green and white box with black letters, instruction sheet, full bottle **6.00**

Ozomulsion, T. A. Slocum Co, New York, NY, "cod liver oil tonic," 7-fl oz brown bottle with gold metal cap and wire closure, 2⅞″ × 1⅞″ × 7¼″ orange and wine box with orange and wine label, codfish swimming in water, name embossed, Spanish and English instruction and advertisement booklet, "improved Jan. 1, 1927," full bottle **8.50**

Peptiron, C. I. Hood Co Laboratories, New York, St. Louis, formerly Lowell, MA, "tonic with digestive aid, stimulant and two laxatives," 50 pills, clear glass cork-stoppered bottle in 3″ × 1½″ × 1″ tan and black box with black letters, instruction and advertisement booklets, pack of two sample pills, full bottle **12.00**

Puretest Brewer's Yeast Tablets, United Drug Co, Boston, St. Louis, USA, "B-complex vitamin" 100 tabs, in 4⅜″ × 2″ × 2¼″ clear glass tapered bottle with white and green label with blue letters, full bottle **5.00**

Rubrafolin, E. R. Squibb & Sons, New York, NY, "vitamin B12 concentrate and folic acid," 100 caps, 3½″ × 1¾″ brown octagonal bottle, 10 caps **8.00**

S.S.S. Tablets with Iron, S.S.S. Co, Atlanta, GA, 20 tabs, 2¾″ × 1½″ small round brown bottle, red, white, and black box with red, white, and black letters, full bottle **5.00**

Tablets Gluferate, Wyeth Inc, Philadelphia, PA, 100 tabs, 1⅞″ × 1⅞″ brown bottle in tan, blue, and white box, full bottle **6.00**

Tamate (Brand of Hematinic with Vitamin B1), The Wm S Merrell Co, Cincinnati, OH, USA, 100 tabs, 2″ × 1⅛″ × 4⅞″ brown bottle, blue and white label with dark blue letters, "founded 1828," full bottle **8.00**

Vi-Litron Drops, U.S. Vitamin Corp, Casimir Funk Laboratories, Inc, New York, NY, 15-cc round brown bottle with dropper in 2⅛″ × 3½″ × 1¼″ light blue and white box with black and white letters, full bottle **5.50**

Vita-Metrazol, Knoll Pharmaceutical Co, Orange, NJ, 100 tabs, 1½″ × 3¼″ round brown bottle, white, black, and yellow label with black and white letters, instruction sheet, full bottle **6.25**

Vitamins A & D Concentrated Capsules, Miller Laboratories Mfg Chemists, Cleveland, OH, 100 caps, 3½″ × 1″ × 1½″ brown bottle, blue and white label with blue letters, ½-full bottle **4.75**

Vitawine, Interstate Labs Inc, Louisville, KY, "iron and vitamin B1 and B2 tonic," 8-fl oz clear bottle in 3⅛″ × 1½″ × 8″ wine,

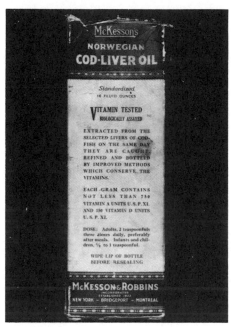

*Norwegian Cod-Liver Oil, McKesson and Robbins Inc, New York, Bridgeport, Montreal, Vitamin A & D tonic, 16-fl oz, 9″ × 3″ × 2″ brown glass bottle with wine and white label with white letters in 9″ × 3″ × 2¼″ wine and white cardboard box, embossed fish on back of bottle, box has no lid, full bottle **11.00***

white, and black box with black and white letters, instruction sheet and advertisement, reorder card, 194_, full bottle **12.00**

White's Aquasperse A, C, D Drops, White Laboratories Inc, Kenilworth, NJ, 15-cc round brown bottle with dropper in 1⅞″ × 3½″ × 1″ white, yellow, and brown box with brown and white letters, full bottle **3.75**

Yeast Foam Tablets with Iron, Consolidated Royal Chem. Corp, Chicago, IL, 60 tabs, brown bottle in 2¼″ × 1¼″ × 3⅝″ yellow, blue, and tan box with black and white letters, instruction sheet, full bottle **10.00**

Zestin, Rhodes Pharmacal Co, Inc, Cleveland, OH, "fortified tonic elixir," 4-fl oz brown bottle in 2½″ × 4¾″ × 1½″ tan, orange, and black box with black and tan letters, full bottle **7.50**

Vermin Remedies

Many years ago children were sent to the school nurse's office and were instructed to sit quietly in a dark room. The nurse would closely examine each child's head with an ultraviolet light to search for lice. If any of the tiny creatures were discovered, the child was sent home. Nyal Larkspur Lotion, a popular product, was applied freely into the hair with the fingertips at night and in the morning for several days. Then the hair was washed with soap and water and a fine-toothed comb used to remove nits from the scalp.

Pin Worm infestation was a common occurrence and all members of the family needed to be treated at the same time. Dr. Thacher's Tablets, a recognized pinworm remedy, contained gentian violet. Infected individuals wore tight-fitting pants at night. All underwear, bed clothes, and towels were to be boiled. Pregnant women, heavy drinkers, and victims of heart, kidney, liver, or intestinal ailments were advised to avoid this product.

The Cenol Company distributed the versatile Pedic Liquid, which destroyed crab body lice, head lice, chiggers, mites, and nits with one application.

Dr. Thacher's Tablets, Allied Drug Products Co, Chattanooga, TN, "a recognized treatment for pin worms," 60 tabs, 2⅛″ × 1¼″ blue glass bottle with gold metal lid in 2¼″ × 1⅜″ × 1⅜″ orange cardboard box with brown letters **6.00**

Frey's Vermifuge, Boyle-Midway Inc, distr, Jersey City, NJ, USA, "for expelling the large roundworms in adults and children, also in puppies and dogs," 1½-fl oz, 3½″ × 1½″ × 1½″ clear glass bottle with red metal lid in 3¾″ × 1½″ × 1½″ yellow cardboard box with black letters **3.00**

Harrison's Lotion, Harrison's Laboratories, Jackson, MS, "effective remedy for germi-

Hokus Pokus, Hirschman Laboratories, San Pedro, CA, "kills all vermin that infest the body," 1 fl oz, 3¼″ × 1¼″ round clear glass bottle with black and gold label with gold letters, gold drawing of magician's head and hands, empty bottle **35.00**

cidal athlete's foot, common ringworm and minor skin irritations," 1-fl oz, 3½″ × 1⅜″ × ¾″ clear glass bottle with black lid in 4½″ × 1½″ × 1″ red and white cardboard box with blue letters **10.00**

Larkspur Lotion, mfr by McKesson & Robbins Inc, New York, NY; Bridgeport, CT, USA, "kills head lice (pediculus capitis) when used as directed," 4-fl oz, 4¾″ × 1⅞″ × 1⅜″ clear glass bottle with red metal lid in 5¾″ × 2¼″ × 1¾″ red and white cardboard box with red letters, sealed bottle **13.00**

Pedic Liquid, Cenol Co, Chicago, IL, USA, "for destroying crab lice, body lice, head lice, chiggers, mites and nits," 4-fl oz, 4¾″ × 1⅝″ brown glass bottle with blue metal lid, orange, blue, and white label with orange, blue, and white letters **6.50**

Sit-i-cide, prepared by the Siticide Co Inc, Commerce, GA, "destroys those itch-mites of scabie-itch with which it comes in contact," 4-fl oz, 4¾" × 1⅞" × 1⅜" clear glass bottle with red metal lid in 5¾" × 2¼" × 1¾" red and white cardboard box with red letters, sealed bottle **13.00**

Women's Health and Hygiene Products

Lydia E. Pinkham has been meeting feminine hygiene needs for nearly a century. Women of all ages have depended on her products' "curative" powers.

Douche powders, estrogenic hormones, pain remedies, sanitary products, suppositories, and vaginal products were all available for "female trouble." Over the generations, each of these products became more "modern" and sophisticated.

DOUCHE POWDERS

The directions on most douche powders strongly advised using the product only once or twice a week unless otherwise directed by a physician. Dutex Retention Douche was promoted as providing a completely new and different principle of douching. The instructions included six steps, which could be mastered after several attempts. Each try would become easier and more effective—a small price to pay for using this modern, dainty method of douching.

In rural areas—far from a drugstore—a woman could find douching instructions on the Lysol bottle.

Hygefem, The Blue Line Chemical Co, St. Louis, MO, 4-oz clear glass bottle in 2⅜" × 4⅛" × 1½" pink with black letters, three pictures of a woman's head and part of shoulder, holding her hand up to her face, full bottle **6.00**

V.A. Douche Powder, Norcliff Labs, Fairfield, CT, 4-oz, 3¼" × 2½" round, knobby,

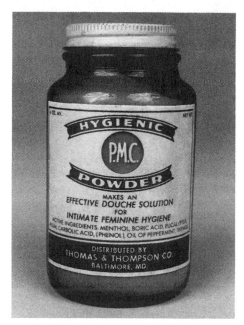

*Hygienic P.M.C. Powder, Thomas & Thompson Co, Baltimore, MD 4-oz, 4¼" × 2¼" round brown bottle with light blue and navy blue label and letters, full bottle **8.75***

clear glass jar, white, silver, blue, and navy label with white and navy letters, full jar **4.75**

ESTROGENIC HORMONES

Ovlin Tablets, Sig: Lab. Inc, Marshall, IL, "conjugated estrogens," 100 tabs, 2⅝" × 1¼" round brown bottle with tan and red label and black and red letters **3.00**

Proluton, Schering Corp, Bloomfield, NJ, "corpus luteum hormone," 1-cc, 3¾" × 2¼" × ¾" tan, brown, black, and yellow box, full box **9.00**

PREGNANCY/LABOR MEDICATIONS

Cotton Root Bark, The Wm. S. Merrell Co, Cincinnati, OH, USA, "uterine stimulant, astringent to increase uterine contractions during pregnancy," 2" × 5¼" round brown cork-stoppered bottle, tan, green, and navy label and letters, picture of a factory on front **15.00**

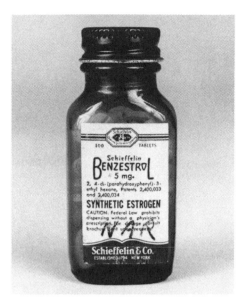

*Benzestrol, Schieffelin & Co, New York, NY, "established 1794," "synthetic estrogen," 100 tabs, 2¼" × ¾" × 1¼" square brown bottle with white and navy label and letters, full bottle **4.25***

VAGINAL PRODUCTS

Cooper Creme, Whittaker Labs Inc, Peekskill, NY, "the original vaginal creme—since 1934," 75-gram yellow tube in 6½" × 2" × 1¼" yellow and black box with black letters, full tube **9.50**

Dr. Pierce's Lotion Tablets, Pierce's Proprietaries Inc, Buffalo, NY; Toronto, ONT, "for preparing douche solution," 28 tabs in round gold tin in 2½" × ¾" × 2½" blue box, signature and picture of Dr. Pierce on one end, instruction sheet, full tin **10.00**

WOMEN'S PAIN REMEDIES

Lydia E. Pinkham's Vegetable Compound was used by women to relieve hot flashes and certain other symptoms associated with the "change of life" (menopause), cramps, and other distress of menstruation. This compound was also used as a uterine sedative and helped bowel regularity.

Chi-Ches-Ters, Chichester Chemical Co, Philadelphia, PA, "pain tablets," 30 tabs, 1⅜" × 2⅜" × 1" red, gold, and black box with black and gold letters, full unopened box **7.00**

WOMEN'S SANITARY PRODUCTS

The Kimberly Clark Company of Neenah, Wisconsin, produced Kotex sanitary napkins in various absorbencies, including regular and super extra absorbent.

Early advertising for Modess proclaimed "Remember, Oh Yes, when you ask for "Modess." It was not all that uncommon for a woman to attempt to follow this advice, become flustered, and ask for a box of "Oh Yesses."

Pictured on the instruction leaflet for early tampons, Nappons, are three women sitting around a table. The woman in the middle holds a Nappon

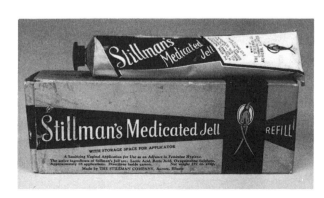

*Stillman's Medicated Jell, The Stillman Co, Aurora, IL, "established 1891," 2½-oz refill tube, white inner box, 6½" × 2⅜" × 1⅛" wine, black, and white outer box with black and white letters, picture of a long-tailed bird on a white circle, full tube **10.00***

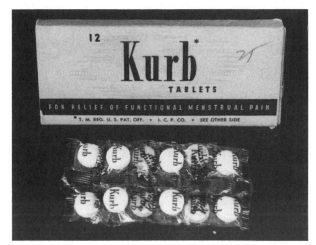

Kurb Tablets, International Cellucotton Product Co, Chicago, IL, "relieves menstrual pain," 12 tabs, in 4¼" × ¼" × 1¾" tan, black, and orange packet, cellophane-wrapped tablets, full box 6.75

Vegetable Compound, Lydia E. Pinkham Medicine Co, Lynn, MA, "relieves 'hot flashes' etc, and monthly cramps, uterine sedative," 14½"-fl oz, 8" × 3" × 1½" clear glass bottle with white label with black letters, embossed name near top of bottle 17.00

in a glass of water. "Now you can see why Nappons give you greater comfort, protection, and security." As the Nappon approached maximum absorbency, the end nearest the removal cord would began to expand and lengthen. When a Nappon was placed properly, the user would notice a gentle pressure against the sphincter muscle. This was a special "time-to-change" feature of Nappons.

Kleinert's Sanitary Brief, Kleinert's, New York, NY, "no sanitary belt needed, waterproof panel," medium size, 27" to 29" waist, 4¼" × 7" × 1" white box **9.00**

Modess Luxury Belt, Personal Products Co, Milltown, NJ, est. 1964, 1"-wide, sizes 22" to 40", 3⅓" × 4" × ⅜" blue, green, and white package, woman dressed in old-fashioned long light blue dress, belt shows through the clear plastic beside her, **5.00**

Modess Vee-Form Napkins, Personal Products Corp, Milltown, NJ, "narrower, deeper, tapered," 12 napkins, 7" × 3⅜" × 7⅞" gold, blue, and white box with gold, blue, and white letters, picture of napkin on back, full box **8.00**

WOMEN'S SUPPOSITORIES

Dr. Pierre's Boro-Pheno-Form, Dr. Pierre Chem Co, Chicago, IL, 12 medicated sup-

Nappons, Nappons Laboratories, Chicago, IL, ten internal napkins 6⅛" × 3⅝" × 1½" in light blue and white box with light blue and white letters, full box **7.00**

Loray Sanitary Shield, Loray Products Inc, Los Angeles, CA, one shield in 6½" × 3½" light blue, medium blue, dark blue, black, and white plastic package with black and blue letters, picture of two women's heads, one embarrassed, one not, full package **5.00**

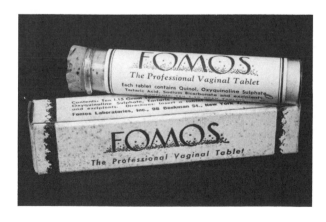

Famos Vaginal Tablet, Fomos Laboratories Inc, New York, NY, ten tabs in glass cork-stoppered vial, 4" × ¾" × ¾" white and wine box with wine letters, instruction sheet, full vial **10.00**

positories in 2″ × 1½″ × 1″ navy blue box, blue and white front and back labels with blue and red letters, full unopened box **9.00**

Orange Blossom Suppositories, Dr. J. A. McGill Co, Chicago, IL, "for the local irritation of simple vaginitis," six suppositories in 2½″ × 1½″ × ¾″ orange slide-top box with black letters, two foil-wrapped individual suppositories **7.50**

Women's Toiletries

Women have always wanted to look their best. Visits to the cosmetic counter at Woolworth's, the drugstore, and boutiques defy the old adage "Beauty is only skin deep." Colors, textures, and products have changed over the decades, but women still continue to keep up with the latest innovations.

Cashmere Bouquet, Talcum Powder, Colgate-Palmolive Co, New York, NY, body powder, "The talc with the fragrance men love," 6½-oz, 6¼″ × 3½″ × 1¼″ pink, white, and blue metal can with red and black letters, full can **15.00**

WOMEN'S BATH POWDERS

Eileen Dusting Powder, Stevens-Wiley, Philadelphia, PA, 8-oz, 5″ × 5″ × 2⅞″ white cardboard box with purple letters, flower print **12.00**

WOMEN'S COLOGNE

Fragrances can be seductive, spicy, woodsy, floral, and feminine. Hypnotique (Max Factor), Gardenia (Park & Tilford), Floral (Adrienne), White Mink, Frosted (Cara Nome), Christmas in July (Minico), and Chanel No. 5 competed for a woman's attention.

The perfume counter lured customers with fragrance-testers. Famous Perfume Typer, which provided sixty-five individual "Nip Bottlettes" could be used individually in the privacy of the home.

Perfume companies were always encouraging women to change perfume scents, and they frequently distributed small complimentary bottles to customers.

Holidays heralded the advent of Christmas bells, slippers, and packages—all with bottles concealed.

Adrienne Floral Essence, Adrienne, Los Angeles, Boston, St. Louis, USA; Toronto, CAN; printed in USA, "a fragrant essence combining the richness and economy of a cologne for lavish use," 4-fl oz, 5″ × 2⅓″ × 1¼″ clear glass bottle with white plastic lid, white and gold label with white and gold letters, full bottle **7.50**

Ben Hur Perfume, Jergens Cincinnati, ¼-fl oz, 2⅛″ × 1½″ × ½″ clear glass bottle with red plastic lid, blue label with black letters, red heart on label, ½-full bottle **6.00**

Chanel No. 5 Spray Cologne, Chanel, Inc, New York distr, 1½-fl oz, 4½″ × 1⅜″ × 1⅜″ black and gold plastic container with black plastic lid over spray top in 4½″ × 1¾″ × 1¾″ white cardboard box with black letters, instruction sheet, full container **11.00**

Christmas in July Cologne, Monico Inc, New York, NY distr, 6-fl oz, 5⅛″ × 2″ clear glass bottle with gold metal lid and white letters, picture of snowflakes, full bottle **9.00**

Coty L'Aimant, New York Parfum, .16-fl oz, 2½″ × ⅝″ clear glass bottle with gold metal lid, black label with gold letters, 2½″ × 2¾″ gold Christmas bell and bow attached, full bottle **12.00**

Coty L'Origan, New York Parfum, .16-fl oz, 2½″ × ⅝″ clear glass bottle with gold metal lid, black label with gold letters, 2¼″ × 3″ gold shoe and bow attached, full bottle **15.00**

Gardenia, Park & Tilford, distr New York City, ½-fl oz, 2⅜″ × 1⅜″ × ¾″ clear glass bottle with blue plastic lid, yellow and green label with black letters in 3″ × 2″ × 1″ clear plastic box, picture of flower, full bottle **8.00**

Hypnotique Spray Mist Cologne, Max Factor, Hollywood, London, Paris, clear glass 2¼″ × 6¼″ bottle with spray top in 7¼″ × 2½″ × 2½″ white cardboard box with black letters, counter fragrance tester "not for resale," full bottle **20.00**

White Mink Frosted Cologne, Cara Nome, distr, Boston, Los Angeles, 3½-oz, 1⅞″ × 3¾″ cloudy glass jar with white metal lid, black letters, full jar **8.00**

Yeasel's Orange Blossom Perfume, N.E. Yeasel Products, St. Cloud, FL, 1-fl oz, 1½″ × 2¼″ orange plastic container with white plastic lid, green and white label with gold letters **5.50**

Your Perfume Typer of Famous Name Perfumes, 3½″ × 4⅝″ × ⅝″ black plastic container with clear plastic snap-top lid, white label with black and pink letters, contents: 65 Nip Bottlettes and perfume guide **20.00**

WOMEN'S COSMETICS

Products for the eyes, lips, and cheeks often were elaborately packaged. At the beginning of World War II, however, manufacturers had to change their packaging to save materials for the war effort. Products of that era were packaged in cardboard rather than in elaborate tins or cobalt bottles.

Eye Makeup

Cosmetically Yours Eye Brow Pencil Refills, Cosmetically Yours, Inc, Yonkers, NY, 1¾″ × ⅜″ clear plastic tube contains four leads on 3¾″ × 3″ white card with red and black letters **6.00**

Maybelline Cream Mascara, Maybelline Co, distr, Chicago, IL, USA, 2¾″ × 1″ × ½″ clear plastic container holds brush and tube of cream on 5″ × 2¾″ white card with red and blue letters **8.00**

Makeup

Cara Nome Backstage Liquid Powder Base, Cara Nome, Boston, Los Angeles, 1-fl oz, 2″ × 2″ × 1¼″ clear glass jar with peach lid, peach and gold label with brown letters **10.00**

Coty DeLuxe Cream Powder, L'Origan Vibrant, New York, Paris, .50-oz, 2⅝″ × ½″ gold and black plastic compact, gold letters **6.50**

Evening in Paris, Bourjois, New York, "harmonized make-up ensemble—this ensemble contains rouge and lipstick selected to harmonize with the face powder shade," 2½-oz, 1½″ × 3½″ blue and silver cardboard container with blue letters, silhouette drawings of people in Paris **20.00**

Woodbury Face Powder Compact Refills, John H. Woodbury, Inc, Cincinnati, OH, ⅓-oz, 2¾″ × 2″ × ¼″ blue cardboard box with blue letters, picture of woman **5.50**

12 refills in 4″ × 2¾″ × 2¼″ brown cardboard box, full box **66.00**

Makeup Applicators

Helen Cornell Deep Pile Powder Puffs, Rexall Drug Co Distr, Los Angeles, Toronto, London, three 2½″ × ¼″ peach-colored puffs in gold, clear, and black plastic cellophane with gold and black letters **5.00**

Plex Cosmetic Sponge, American Sponge & Chamois Co Inc, New York, "downy soft when moist," 2¾" × 2¼" × ¼" yellow sponge in blue, white, and clear cellophane with black, white, and red letters **3.75**

Rouge

Creme Rouge, Max Factor & Co, Hollywood, CA, 2.5-grams, 1⅝" × ⅜" white plastic container with gold and black letters **6.00**

WOMEN'S DEODORANT

Next to feminine hygiene protection, no other pharmaceutical product was so discreet as deodorant. "New" Hush contained an exclusive cream applicator. (An introductory-size bottle of Tame Cream Rinse was included as a gift.) Sweetheart Deodorant Pads and the popular Fresh, Mum, and Dryad all kept underarms dry and odor-free.

Hush Deodorant, 1959 The Gillette Co, Chicago, IL, made in USA, "the new deodorant developed to control even stubborn cases of perspiration and odor," 1.35-oz, 3¾" × 1½" white plastic container with white plastic lid in 4¼" × 3¾" × 1½" blue, white, and yellow cardboard box with white, black, and blue letters, sample Tame cream rinse, 1.5-fl oz, 3½" × 1⅜" clear glass bottle with blue plastic lid **8.75**

Quest All-Purpose Deodorant, distr, by International Cellucotton Products Co, Chicago, IL, USA, "completely destroys body odors," 2-oz, 4½" × 1⅝" metal container with metal lid over shaker top, brown and white label with brown and white letters, ½-full container **5.00**

Sutton Cream Deodorant, distr by Sutton Cosmetics, Kenilworth, NJ, "stops underarm odor instantly, checks perspiration and helps keep you dry," 1.05-oz, 1" × 2¼" white glass container with blue and white metal lid in 2½" × 2½" × 1⅜" blue and white cardboard box with blue and white letters, picture of snowflake, full container **8.00**

Sweetheart Deodorant Pads, distr by Sweetheart Cosmetic, Boston, MA, USA, div of Manhattan Soap Co, Inc, "underarms will keep dry and odorless," 35 pads in 1⅞" × 2⅓" clear glass jar with red and white metal lid, red and white label with red and white letters, pictures of hearts and angel, full jar **8.00**

WOMEN'S HAIR-CARE PRODUCTS

Women could literally change their looks with the flip of a bottle, the use of a curling iron, or the application of a permanent. A meticulous shear could convert a beehive belle of the 1950s into a pixie of the 1960s.

Gillette's Self End Paper Permanent provided waves without lotion. Richard Hudnut's Home Permanent included "ample curling rods for a complete permanent." Women would reach for Lustre-Creme Hair Dressing with Lanolin if they wanted to add gleaming highlights to the hair. Date Line Hair Dressing was designed especially for teenage girls.

Hair Color

One of the earliest hair-coloring products was "Powdered Henna" (Egyptian) for tinting auburn hair, distributed by The Russ & Heeble Co. of Indianapolis.

Colorinse by Nestlé was available in attractive packages and contained easy-to-apply powders. The Noreen Company's individual capsules contained the exact amount needed for each rinse.

Blondex Shampoo, prepared by Swedish Shampoo Laboratories, New York, NY, "Blondex is made especially for blond hair," three packets in 4½" × 3" × ½" blue and yellow cardboard box, blue and white letters, full box **3.00**

Canute Water, bottled and distributed by The Canute Co, Santa Barbara, CA, USA, "scientifically recolors bleached, faded and gray hair," 5⅛" × 2⅞" × 1¼" orange, white, and black box with black and white letters, full unopened box **8.00**

Kolor-Bak, Consolidated Royal Chemical Corp, Chicago, IL, "a solution for artificially coloring gray hair," 8-oz, 6" × 2" brown glass bottle with brown plastic lid, orange, black, and white label with orange and black letters, picture of woman, full bottle **10.00**

Nestlé Colorinse, Nestlé-LeMur, New York, NY, "use after every shampoo, gives glamorous color highlights, imparts beautiful new sheen," six rinses, 3½" × 5¼" × ½" white, blue, and pink cardboard box with yellow, white, and black letters, picture of woman, instruction sheet, full box **7.00**

Nestlé Colortin, Nestlé-LeMur, London, New York, Toronto, "gives radiant new color instantly, not a permanent dye," six capsules in 5¼" × 3⅜" × ½" yellow, white, and pink cardboard box with windows, black and pink letters, instruction sheet, picture of woman, full box **4.25**

Noreen Color Hair Rinse, Lehn & Fink Products Corp, Bloomfield, NJ, "glorifies your hair with abundant temporary color, eight color-rinse capsules in 5¼" × 1⅛" × 1⅛" white pink, and red cardboard box with cellophane window, black letters, full box **4.00**

Powdered Henna, The Rush & Hebble Co, Indianapolis, IN, "for tinting the hair auburn and titian, 2-oz, 2½" × 2¼" clear glass jar with white metal lid, yellow and white label with black letters, full jar **6.50**

Hair Curling and Setting

Charles Antell Hair Spray with Lanolin, Charles Antell, Inc, Distributor, Baltimore, MD, "controls stray ends and wisps of hair, gives body to waves, protects hair from wind and rain, makes hair lovely, lustrous and manageable," 2½-oz, 3¾" × 2⅛" metal can with blue plastic lid, gold, blue, and white label with blue and white letters, empty can **5.00**

Date Line Hair Dressing and Conditioner, Women's Division, The Mennen Co, Morristown, NJ: Toronto, ONT, "a greaseless medicated conditioner specially for-

mulated to help hair problems," 6½" × 6¼" × 2⅛" metal canister with blue plastic pump top, pink and white label with blue, pink, and white letters, picture of dove and heart, full canister **7.50**

Dr. Ellis Curlast Wave Set, Ar. Winarick Inc, New York, NY, "for soft, natural waves and pincurls," 4¾-fl oz, 5" × 2¼" × 1" clear glass bottle with silver metal lid, white and black label with black, gold, and white letters, picture of woman, empty bottle **10.00**

Lustre-Creme Hair Dressing, Kay Daumit Division, Colgate-Palmolive Co Licensee, 300 Park Ave, New York, NY, "to add gleaming highlights to the hair," 1¾-fl oz, 3¾" × 1½" clear glass bottle with blue plastic lid, blue letters, full bottle **5.00**

New Self End Paper Permanent, The Gillette Co, Chicago, IL, made in USA, "waves without lotion," kit includes papers, applicator, and neutralizer in 4¼" × 5¼" × 2⅛" pink, green, blue, and white cardboard box with black, green, blue, and pink letters, full kit **12.00**

Richard Hudnut Home Permanent Plastic Curling Rods, Richard Hudnut, New York, Paris, "ample curling rods for a complete permanent," 60 curling rods in 3½" × 4½" × 1¾" gray and black cardboard box with yellow, white, and black letters, full box **12.00**

Hair Nets

Hair nets often were synthetic and machine made, but some were handmade of real hair!

Collecting hint: Many of these paper packages contained pictures with excellent graphics. Display the packages in picture frames and keep the hair net in the package for authenticity.

Cupid Fine Mesh Net, The Glemby Co Inc, "a strongly woven small mesh net, made to securely hold hair in place while worn," 6½" × 5" white envelope with blue letters, picture of woman, empty envelope **6.00**

Duro Belle Human Hair Net, National Trading Co, Chicago, IL, 4½″ × 5¾″ blue and orange envelope with blue and orange letters, drawings of women, full envelope **7.50**

Flamingo Hair Net, 1958 Flamingo Products, Inc, Danville, IL, Trade Mark Reg, made in USA, 6½″ × 3½″ pink and white envelope with brown and pink letters, picture of woman, full envelope **2.75**

Hair-Styling Accessories

The Westinghouse Electric Curling Iron was a boon to women who had previously depended on the old-fashioned wooden-handled curling irons that needed to be reheated frequently. No longer would Lady Beautiful Bobby Pins be misplaced when they could be kept in a Sav-UR-Clip Tray! Tip Top curlers could be kept in their own Tip Top Curler Apron. Its drawstring closure converted the curler apron into a handy curler caddy as well.

Capri Automatic Hair Curler, by L & R Lenzi, Inc, Neptune, NJ, 5¼″ × 4¾″ × ½″ pink plastic curler in 5⅛″ × 4⅝″ × ⅝″ red, white, and black cardboard box with red, white, and black letters **12.00**

Clairol Kindness Heat Retaining Rollers, Underwriter Laboratories, Inc, Clairol Inc, New York, NY distributors, "to create any hairstyle in minutes," 5″ × 4″ × 1½″ blue and white cardboard cellophane-wrapped package with blue and black letters, unopened one-roller package **8.50**

Goody Magnetic Rollers, H. Goodham & Sons, Inc, New York, 10¼″ × 5½″ × 1½″ pink and white cardboard cellophane-sealed package with black, white, and pink letters **8.75**

Hold Bob Automatic Insert-o-pin Curler, created and made only by The Hump Hairpin Mfg Co, 4¾″ × ½″ gold metal and red plastic curler with three hairpins on orange and yellow card 7″ × 5½″ booklet, black and orange letters **10.00**

Holdette Non-Slip Ring Comb, a Tilco Product, 1½″ × 1⅜″ blue plastic comb on 4″ × 3¾″ blue and white card with blue letters **1.75**

Lady Ellen Hollywood Klippies, The Kaynar Co, Los Angeles, Chicago, New York, assembled in Mexico, "for every hair setting need," 6¾″ × 4¼″ yellow, black, green, white, and blue card with red, white, and yellow letters, almost-full nine-pack **1.50**

Sav-Ur-Clip Tray, Sole Distributor Charles G. Spilo, Los Angeles, CA, 3¾″ × 4″ × 3″ yellow plastic tray in 4¾″ × 4⅛″ × 3″ blue and white cardboard box with blue and white letters **15.00**

Solo French Roll Foundation, Solo Products Corp, New York, 7¼″ × 4⅛″ red and yellow card with black and white letters, four giant bob pins **3.75**

Tip-Top Curler Apron, Tip-Top Products Co, Omaha, NE, mfr of World's Finest Hair Curlers and Notions Specialties, 9″ × 4″ × 1″ plastic package with 7¼″ × 3¾″ purple and black card with red and black letters, picture of woman **10.00**

Tip-Top Curlers, Tip-Top Products Co, Omaha, NE, mfr of World's Finest Hair Curlers and Notions Specialties, six-pack, 6¼″ × 3¾″ gray and blue cardboard package with red, blue, and white letters, full plastic-wrapped package **10.50**

Vassar Beautifying Butterflies, The Vassar Corp, New York, NY, two-pack decorative hair pins on 4″ × 4½″ gold card with black letters, full card **3.75**

Vicky Victory Hairpin Kit, Smith Victory Corp, Buffalo, New York, 1¾″ × 2¼″ × ½″ green, blue, and white cardboard box with blue and white letters **2.25**

Westinghouse Electric Curling Iron, 9″ × 1″ metal curling iron with black plastic handle and 70″ cord in 3″ × 9½″ × 1¾″ white cardboard box, instruction sheet **23.00**

Shampoo

The Keifer-Stewart Company of Indianapolis recommended that if a person contracted a cold easily after washing the hair, an application of Old

Gibralter Hair Tonic would be in order. This scalp astringent protected the user from exposure, imparted a brilliance and smoothness to the hair, and counteracted falling hair and dandruff.

Proctor and Gamble's Drene left the hair shining with no cloudy film. All the natural beauty would be reflected whenever a woman shook her tresses. Tame, White Rain, and Halo were popular in the 1950s. Commercials advertising these products were often interspersed throughout "Your Hit Parade," "I've Got a Secret," and "The Gary Moore Show."

One product that left its impression on hair care in the 1960s was "Minipoo Dry Shampoo." A pert, properly coiffed young woman on the package modeled a smooth pageboy with bangs. In less than ten minutes her hair would be squeaky clean without wetting or resetting.

Cham-Kana Shampoo, Du-Kana, Paris, New York, "the original quinine shampoo method for preserving youthful hair," 5¼" × 4¼" paper envelope, yellow and red label with black letters, picture of cupids and a woman, instruction sheet **3.00**

DeWitt's Saponified Coconut Oil Shampoo, mfr by E. C. DeWitt & Co Inc, Chicago, IL, 4-fl oz, 4½" × 1¾" brown glass bottle with black plastic lid in 4½" × 2" × 2" orange, white, and green cardboard box with black letters, instruction sheet, picture of woman, ½-full bottle **15.00**

Harade, Harade Co, New York, Atlanta, "a scientific preparation and a food for the scalp invigorates and beautifies the hair giving it a natural and healthy appearance," 3-oz, 2⅞" × 2½" × 1¼" metal container, orange and gold label with orange and gold letters **8.50**

Marrow's Mar-O-Oil Shampoo, Marrow's Inc, Chicago, IL, Made in USA, "a combination of oils we recommend for normal, dry or oily hair," 2-fl oz, 4½" × 1¾" clear glass bottle with red metal lid in 4⅝" × 2" × 2"

red and black cardboard box with black letters, picture of woman, ½-full bottle **21.00**

Minipoo Dry Shampoo, Cosmetic Distr, Jersey City, NJ, "new 10 minute way to clean hair," 3-oz, 5⅛" × 2¼" shaker container, pink and black label with black, white, and pink letters, picture of woman **8.50**

Old Gibraltar Opal Shampoo, prepared by Kiefer-Stewart Co, Indianapolis, IN, "should be used regularly whenever hair and scalp need a thorough cleansing," 6¼" × 1¾" × 1⅛" clear glass bottle with cork lid in 6½" × 2" × 1½" brown cardboard box with blue letters, picture of woman washing hair **10.00**

Rexall New Awakening Lemon Shampoo, 3½-fl oz, 6¼" × 2¼" × ½" clear plastic bottle with yellow plastic lid, green, white, and yellow label with green and white letters, ½-full bottle **6.50**

Tame Creme Rinse, the Toni Co, Chicago, A Div of The Gillette Co, made in USA, "ends snarls and tangles, leaves hair soft, manageable, conditions dry, flyaway hair," 1.5-fl oz, 3½" × 1⅜" clear glass bottle with pale blue lid and green letters, almost-full introductory-size bottle **6.00**

White Rain Lotion Shampoo, by Toni, The Gillette Co, Chicago, IL, 1½-fl oz, 4¾" × 2" × ¾" clear glass bottle with blue plastic lid, blue and white label with blue letters, ¾-full bottle **8.00**

WOMEN'S LOTIONS AND CREAMS

Hinds Honey & Almond Fragrance Cream endured for several generations, and Pacquin's, Cashmere Bouquet, Jergen's, and Pond's practically became household staples.

Campana Italian Balm, Campana Corp, Batavia, IL, "world's finest lotion," 4-fl oz, 5¾" × 2¼" × 1¼" clear glass bottle with white plastic lid, gold and white label with gold and green letters **7.00**

Cara Nome Deep Cleansing Lotion, Rexall, Los Angeles, Toronto, made in USA, 4-fl oz, 5" × 1¾" clear glass bottle with white plastic lid, white label with gold letters **9.00**

Cashmere Bouquet, Colgate-Palmolive-Peet Co, Jersey City, NJ, "cold cream for cleansing," $9/16$-oz $1\frac{7}{8}'' \times 1\frac{1}{4}''$ white glass jar with orange and white metal lid, brown label with black and orange letters **8.50**

Derma Fresh Complexion Lotion, Alberto-Culver Co, Melrose Park, IL, "cleans, medicates, moisturizes," 6-fl oz, $7'' \times 2\frac{1}{4}'' \times 1\frac{1}{2}''$ clear glass bottle with blue plastic lid, blue label with silver and white letters, almost-full bottle **8.00**

Desert Flower, Hand & Body Lotion, Shulton, Inc, Clifton, NJ, Toronto, 3.5-fl oz, $6'' \times 1\frac{3}{4}''$ clear glass bottle with white plastic pump lid, white plastic bottle holder, in $5\frac{1}{4}'' \times 3'' \times 2''$ white cardboard box with black letters, demonstrater **15.00**

DeWitt's Lanolized Skin Creme, E. C. DeWitt & Co, Inc, Chicago, IL, 4-fl oz, $5\frac{1}{2}'' \times 2\frac{1}{4}'' \times 1''$ clear glass bottle with white plastic lid, pink and white label with blue letters, almost-full bottle **6.00**

Espey's Fragrant Cream, distr by J. E. Espey Co, Pasadena, CA, "a lotion for the skin," 4-fl oz, $4\frac{1}{2}'' \times 1\frac{3}{4}'' \times 1\frac{3}{4}''$ clear glass bottle with black plastic lid, black and white label with black letters **8.00**

Hinds Honey & Almond Fragrance Cream, Lehn & Fink Products Corp, Bloomfield, NJ, 4-fl oz, $4\frac{1}{2}'' \times 2''$ white plastic bottle with pink plastic lid with pink letters, **10.00**

Lady Esther, Lady Esther, Ltd, Chicago, IL, made in USA, "cleanses, softens, tones, satinizes," $1\frac{4}{5}$-oz, $2\frac{1}{4}'' \times 1\frac{3}{4}''$ white glass jar with pink metal lid, pink label with white letters **10.00**

La Joie De Vivre, Elizabeth Arden, New York, London, Paris, "a rich emollient cream to be used particularly on areas with a tendency to lines," $15/16$-oz, $2'' \times 1\frac{1}{2}''$ pink glass jar with white metal lid, silver label with black letters **4.00**

Lov'ere Hand Creme, Lenwells, Inc, Distr, Chicago, IL, "use Lov-ere before or after exposure to water, wind, or unusual work conditions," 4-oz, $2'' \times 2\frac{5}{8}''$ white glass jar with white metal lid with green letters **2.00**

Mary Lowell Velvet Peach Hand Lotion, House of Lowell Inc, Greenville, OH, 1.25-fl oz, $3'' \times 1\frac{3}{4}''$ clear glass bottle with black and white metal lid with handle, embossed, black letters **20.00**

Nylotis Disappearing Cream, Nyal Co distr, Detroit, "for whitening and softening the skin," 3-oz, $2\frac{1}{2}'' \times 2'' \times 2''$ white glass jar with silver metal lid, black, green and pink label with blue letters **14.00**

Pond's Vanishing Creme Foundation, Pond's Extract Co, New York, "smooths, holds powder, protects," 6.9-oz, $2\frac{7}{8}'' \times 3''$ white glass jar with blue metal lid, white label with black letters, full jar **6.75**

Tissue Cream, Vivian Shaw, New York, $1\frac{1}{4}'' \times 1\frac{1}{2}''$ white glass jar with silver metal lid, silver label with black letters **7.00**

Woodbury All-Purpose Cream, $3'' \times 3\frac{1}{2}''$ white glass jar with yellow metal lid, peach and gold label with red letters **8.75**

CHAPTER THREE

A Sampling of Drug and Chemical Companies and Their Products

Many collectors specialize in vintage items from a specific drug or chemical company. It is not unusual to find a person working for Eli Lilly who is looking for bottles of a specific product (with complete labels) from the company's inception to the present. For this chemical company, insulin would be an excellent representative product.

The alphabetical list of chemical and drug companies that follows is by no means exhaustive. It is meant as a starting point and to show the diversity of collecting possibilities. Following the list, at least one product from each company is described and depicted.

American Drug Industries, Inc
The Antikamnia Remedy Co
Blackstone Products Co, Inc

Bristol-Myers Co
Eli Lilly & Co
Empire Laboratories
Irwin, Neisler & Co
Kiefer-Stewart Co
Leach Chemical Co
Lloyd Brothers, Pharmacists, Inc
Magnus, Mabee and Reynard Inc
Mallinckrodt Chemical Works
McKesson & Robbins Inc
Merck & Co, Inc
Nelson Baker & Co, Inc
Parke, Davis & Co
Rexall Drug Company
Royal Mfg Co
The Tilden Co
United Drug Company
United-Rexall Drug Company
Walgreen Co
William R. Warner & Co, Inc

*Spermaceti, **American Drug Industries,** Inc, Chicago, IL, used in making cosmetics, ointments, candles, etc., 1-lb, 4¾" × 5" round blue and tan cardboard box, white and navy label with white and navy lettering, ¾-full box **10.00***

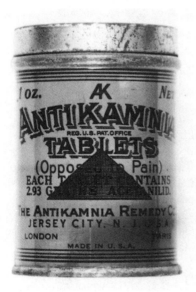

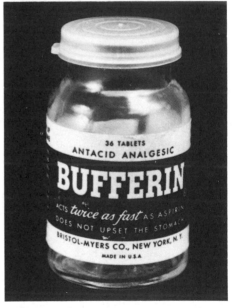

*Antikamnia Tablets, **The Antikamnia Remedy Co,** Jersey City, NJ, USA, analgesic, anodyne, antipyretic, "opposed to pain," 1-oz, 2¼" × 1½" round red tin with gold cap and black letters, full tin **20.00***

*Bufferin, **Bristol-Myers Co,** New York, NY, "for fast, safe pain relief. Acts twice as fast as aspirin," 36 tabs, 2⅜" × 1⅜" round clear glass bottle, navy and white label with navy and white letters, plastic cap, empty bottle **6.00***

Blackstone's Asper-
tane, **Blackstone Products
Co, Inc,** New York, NY, pain
relief, 12 tabs, 1⅜" × 1¾" ×
¼" blue-green tin with black
and white letters, full tin **4.50**

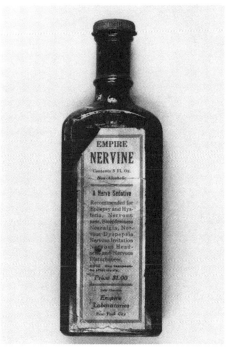

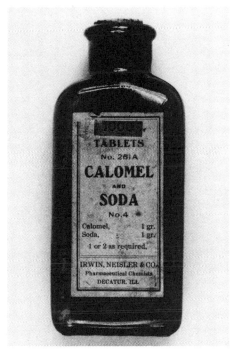

Nervine, **Empire Laboratories,** New York
City, NY, nerve sedative, "Recommended for
Epilepsy and Hysteria, Nervousness . . . Nervous Irritation, Nervous Headache, and
Nervous Disturbances," 8-fl oz, 8¾" × 2¾"
× 1⅜" clear glass bottle, dirty white label
with black letters, ⅓-full bottle **12.00**

Calomel and Soda, **Irwin, Neisler & Co,**
Decatur, IL, cathartic, 1,000 tabs, 5¼" ×
2¼" × 1½" brown glass, cork-stoppered
bottle, tan label with black lettering, ½-full
bottle **24.00**

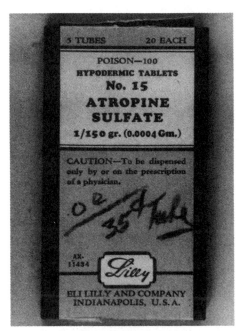

Atropine Sulfate, **Eli Lilly & Co,** Indianapolis, IN, "Hypodermic Tablets," 5 tubes, 3" × ¼" amber glass, cork-stoppered tube, red and white label with red letters, in 3¼" × 1⅞" × ½" green cardboard box with red, white, and yellow label and red letters, slidetop box, empty tube **32.00**

Ichthammol, N.F., **Eli Lilly & Co,** Indianapolis, IN, USA, ointment thought to possess anodyne, antigonorrheal and antiseptic action, 1-lb, 4½" × 4" round textured dark brown glass jar, olive green and white label with black and red lettering, ½-full jar **21.00**

Licorice Compound, **Eli Lilly & Co,** Indianapolis, IN, "for making brown mixture," 1-pt, 7⅞" × 3" × 2" brown glass bottle, green, white, and black label with red and black letters, ⅛-full bottle **18.00**

Sulfadiazine and Tannic Acid Jelly, **Eli Lilly & Co,** Indianapolis, IN, used in treating certain infections, "WARNING this drug may cause severe toxic reactions and irreparable damage. Constant supervision of the patient is essential," 1-oz, 4½" × 1" aluminum tube with green, white, and black label and red and black letters, in 4½" × 1½" × 1" light blue cardboard box in 4¾" × 6" × 4" tan cardboard display box with light blue, black, and white label and black and red letters, 11 full boxed tubes in display box, full display **165.00**

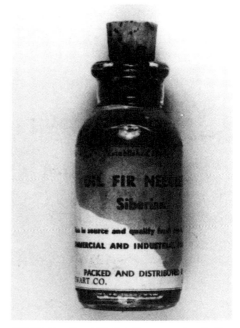

Oil Fir Needles, **Kiefer-Stewart Co,** Indianapolis, IN, disinfectant, "Siberian, differs in source and quality from the U.S.P. oil," 1-fl oz, 3" × 1¼" clear round glass, corkstoppered bottle, white label with black letters, full bottle **18.00**

Oil of Pine, **Leach Chemical Co,** Cincinnati, OH; Windsor, Ontario, healing, "The Healing Properties of the Pines are known throughout the world," ½-oz, 3¼" × 1" wooden cylinder with black and red label and letters, picture of pine trees and log cabin, unopened cylinder **18.00**

Lloyd's Toxirhus, **Lloyd Brothers, Pharmacists, Inc,** Cincinnati, OH, for prophylaxis, poison ivy, and dermatitis, "Alcohol 78 percent," 1-fl oz, 4" × 1⅛" × 1⅛" dark brown glass bottle with dropper cap, white label with red and green lettering, 4½" × 1¼" × 1¼" orange, black, and white box with same label as on bottle, empty bottle **22.00**

Lloyd's Mulleinated Oil, **Lloyd Brothers, Pharmacists Inc,** Cincinnati, OH, treatment of simple earache, 1-fl oz, 3½" × 1¼" × ¾" dark green glass, cork-stoppered bottle, black lettering and green trim on yellow label in 3⅝" × 1½" × 1" white box with black lettering, unopened **26.00**

Sassafras Oil Replacement, **Magnus, Mabee & Reynard,** New York, NY, USA, "an artificial flavor (safrol free)," 4-fl oz, 5" × 1¾" round brown bottle, brown, white and green label with black and white letters, FOOD GRADE, empty bottle **7.50**

Pinotol, **McKesson & Robbins Inc,** *New York, USA, general disinfectant, 3-fl oz, 4½″ × 1¾″ round clear glass bottle, brown label with brown and white lettering, established 1833, ¾-full bottle* **30.00**

Elixir of Phenobarbital, **Nelson Baker & Co,** *Inc, New York, NY, Los Angeles, CA, sedative, "warning—may be habit forming," 1-fl gal, 5½″ × 13″ round brown bottle, tan and red label with red lettering, empty bottle* **27.00**

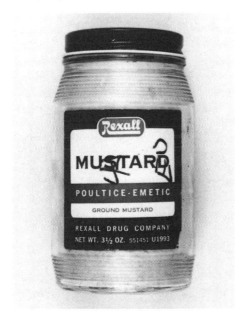

Mustard, **Rexall Drug Company,** *Los Angeles, St. Louis, Boston, USA; Toronto, Canada, Ptd in USA, poultice, emetic, 3½-oz, 4¼″ × 2¼″ clear glass jar with blue metal lid, red, white, and blue label with blue and white letters, full jar* **6.50**

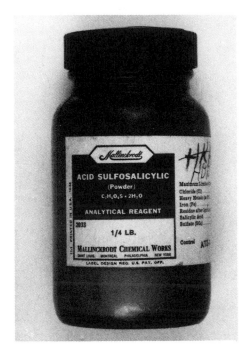

Arsenic Sulphide Yellow, **Mallinckrodt Chemical Works,** *St. Louis, New York, disinfectant "orpiment," 1-oz, 2¼" × 1¼" round brown glass, cork-stoppered bottle, tan and black label with black letters, full bottle* **20.00**

Acid Sulfosalicyclic, **Mallinckrodt Chemical Works,** *St. Louis, Montreal, Philadelphia, New York, kills bacteria and relieves pain, powder, ¼-lb, 4" × 2¼" round brown glass bottle, tan and black label with black letters, ¾-full bottle* **14.00**

Calcium Sulphocarbolate, **Mallinckrodt Chemical Works,** *St. Louis, Montreal, New York, Philadelphia, antiseptic and disinfectant, "fine chemicals—the standard for half a century," ¼-lb, 3⅜" × 2½" round tan cardboard container, tan and black label with black letters, full sealed container* **15.00**

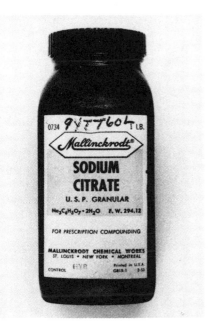

Sodium Citrate, **Mallinckrodt Chemical Works,** St. Louis, New York, Montreal, for prescription compounding, 1-lb, 5¾" × 2¼" × 3½" brown glass bottle with black, blue, and white label and black letters, ½-full bottle **16.00**

Calomel Precipitated, **Mallinckrodt Chemical Works,** St. Louis, Montreal, Philadelphia, New York, purgative, "impalpable powder-mild mercurous chloride," 1-lb, 6" × 2¾" round black glass bottle, tan and black label with black letters, ¼"-full bottle **18.00**

Saxon Sweet Spirit of Nitre, N.F., **Royal Mfg, Co,** Duquesne, PA, diuretic, 1-fl oz, 3¾" × 1½" × ⅞" brown bottle in 4¼" × 1½" × ⅞" navy and white cardboard box with navy and white letters, cutout window in front of box shows bottle label, empty bottle **3.00**

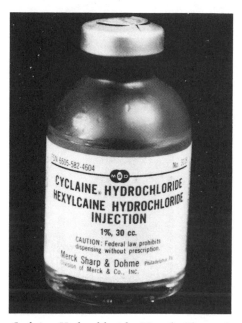

Acid Tannic Merck, **Merck & Co. Inc,** Rahway, NJ, used in tanning, dyeing, medicine, etc., "U.S.P. Fluffy," ¼-lb, 7" × 3¾" round brown glass bottle, tan label with black letters, full bottle **18.00**

Cyclaine Hydrochloride, **Merck, Sharp & Dohme, Div of Merck & Co,** Inc, Philadelphia, PA, minor block anesthesia only, "injection," 30-cc, 2¾" × 1½" clear glass vial, white and navy label with navy lettering in 2¾" × 1⅝" × 1⅝" navy and white cardboard box with navy lettering, no top on box, full, unopened vial **12.00**

Potassium Oxalate, **Merck & Co, Inc,** poisonous acid, used in dyeing, bleaching, etc., ¼-lb, 3½" × 2" round cardboard and metal container, tan and red label with red letters, full container **14.00**

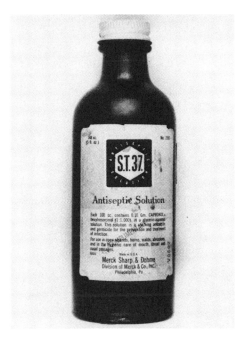

S.T. 37 Antiseptic Solution, **Merck, Sharp & Dohme, Div of Merck & Co** Inc, Philadelphia, PA, for the prevention and treatment of infection, 5-fl oz, 5½" × 2" round blue glass bottle, tan, white, and navy label with navy lettering, "Complimentary" written in red on label, full bottle **8.50**

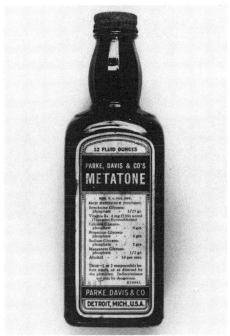

Metatone, **Parke, Davis & Co,** Detroit, MI, tonic, "indiscriminate use may be dangerous," 12-fl oz, 7½" × 2⅜" × 2⅜" clear glass bottle, wine and tan label with wine and tan letters, full bottle **15.00**

Rhubarb and Ipecac Compound, **Parke, Davis & Co,** Detroit, MI, diarrhea and upset stomach, "Roosevelt Hospital," 1,000 compressed tabs 8" × 3" × 1¾" in brown glass cork-stoppered bottle, tan label with black letters, empty bottle **28.00**

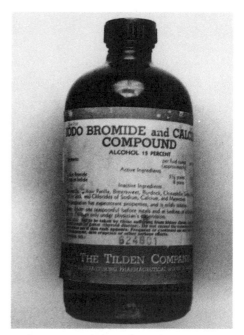

Puretest Sugar of Milk, **United Drug Company,** Boston, St. Louis, USA, "for the preparation of 'modified milk' for infant feeding and for the diet of invalids," 1-lb, 6½" × 3" cardboard container, blue and white label with blue and white letters, full container **30.00**

Iodo Bromide and Calcium Compound, **The Tilden Co,** New Lebanon, NY; St. Louis, MO, sedative, 1-pt, 6¾" × 2⅞" round dark brown bottle, tan label with brown letters, ⅔-full bottle **17.00**

Spirit of Peppermint-U.S.P. **Walgreen Co,** Chicago, IL, flavoring, 1-fl pt, 7¼" × 3" round brown glass bottle with black and white label with black lettering, picture of a mortar and pestle on face of label, ¼-full bottle **20.00**

Defender Throat and Nasal Atomizer, **United-Rexall Drug Company,** Los Angeles, Boston, St. Louis, Toronto, "may be used with aqueous, alcoholic and light oil solutions, especially suited for spraying ephedrine solution," 3" × 1½" × 1" green glass bottle with black metal lid and metal sprayer top in 4¼" × 4¼" × 1¾" blue and white cardboard box with red and blue letters **14.0**

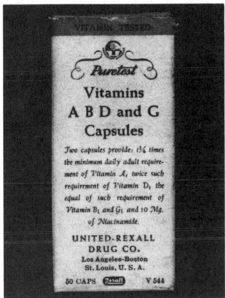

Puretest Vitamins A B D & G Capsules, **United-Rexall Drug Company,** Los Angeles, Boston, St. Louis, USA, "two capsules provide 1¼ times the minimum daily adult requirement of Vitamin A, twice such requirement of Vitamin D, the equal of such requirement of Vitamin B₁ and G₁ and 10 mg of niacinamide," 50 caps, 3" × 1¼" × 1" brown glass bottle with white metal lid in 3⅛" × 1⅝" × 1" green and white cardboard box with blue letters, full bottle **8.75**

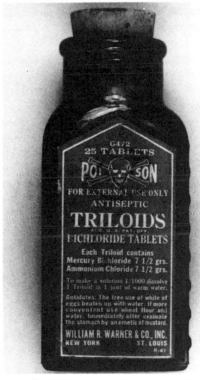

Triloids, **William R. Warner & Co Inc,** New York, NY, St. Louis, MO, antiseptic, 25 tabs, 3½" × 1½" × 1½" cobalt blue glass trianguler cork-stoppered bottle with red label with white letters, the word "poison" embossed on sides, full bottle **35.00**

CHAPTER FOUR

Sample Collections

Developing a vintage pharmaceutical collection requires time, money, discretion, and finesse. While each collector has (or will develop) his or her own idea about what constitutes a collection, most find it useful to compare notes. Here I've provided examples of what I would consider (1) a collection of authentic but contemporary items, (2) a collection of inexpensive items, (3) a collection of moderately priced items, and (4) a collection of expensive items. The four collections are merely examples—places to start—and should be used for inspiration, not exact imitation.

Collection #1
Authentic but Contemporary Items

Pharmaceutical companies continue to give away items that represent their products. Unlike vintage advertising items, these giveaways have very little intrinsic value.

The recipient of these gifts may choose to keep them for potential value, display them for what they are, or give them away.

William Procter Jr. advertising mortar and pestle plaque "secundum arterm," 4" × 4" × ⅓" pot-metal plaque (brassy finish), William Procter (or another doctor) and office room embossed on face of plaque **7.50**

Tinactin advertising 8" × 2¾" round clear glass jar, red and silver label with red letters, empty jar **15.00**

Augmentin and Amoxil advertising medicine measurer, BeeCham Laboratories, Bristol, TN, measure of liquid medicine, "amoxicillin/clavulanate potassium," 8-fl oz or 250-ml, 6½" × 3" round clear and black plastic tapered measurer with red and white letters **6.00**

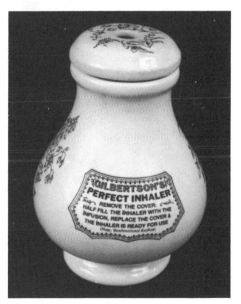

Gilbertson's Perfect Inhaler, Eli Lilly & Co, Indianapolis, IN, relief for bronchial and throat affections, "Note—nonfunctional replica," 1 cup, 5" × 4" round cream, green, and black ceramic tapered jar, black and cream label painted on jar, black letters, "The Story of Inhalers" information sheet enclosed in jar **45.00**

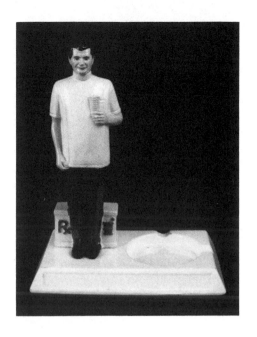

Pharmacy advertising ashtrays, E. R. Squibb & Sons, New York, NY, ashtray, 11" × 8½" × 5⅜" cream, blue, black, gold, and pink ceramic ashtray, yellow label with black letters, figure of pharmacist in uniform holding medicine measurer **35.00**

Collection #2
An Inexpensive Collection

Many pharmaceutical labels can be found for less than a dollar. The labels may be framed, mounted in albums, or affixed to clear or colored bottles. (**Collecting hint:** If the color of the original medication can be determined, fill the bottles with liquid of the same color for authenticity. For example, compound extract of vanilla would be brown, while pink nose drops would be a shade of pink. Look for antique bottles at drugstore supply houses.)

The word "poison" is synonymous with the word "collectible." The skull and crossbones make a label even more desirable.

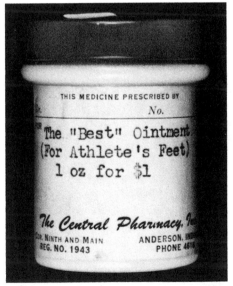

The "Best" Ointment, The Central Pharmacy, Inc, Anderson, IN, athlete's foot ointment, 2-oz, round 2½" × 1⅞" milk glass jar, black and white label with black letters, plastic cap, full jar **6.00**

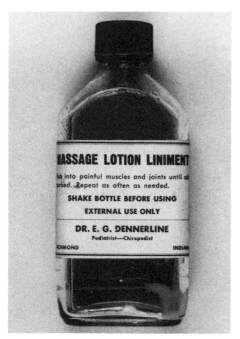

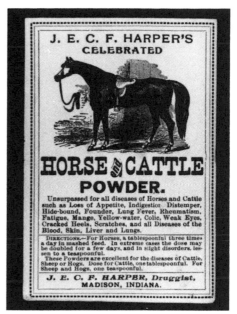

Massage Lotion Liniment, Dr. E. G. Dennerline, Podiatrist-Chiropodist, Richmond, IN, rub for painful muscles and joints, 140-cc, 5½" × 2¼" × 1½" clear glass bottle, navy and white label with navy letters, 20 cc left in bottle **10.00**

Horse and Cattle Powder, label, J.E.C.F. Harper, Druggist, Madison, IN, label to be put on medicine bottle, 3¾" × 2⅝" black and white paper label, picture of a horse, black letters **3.75**

Matchbook Collector, Whitman Publishing Co, no address, holder for matchbook covers, Copyright 1939, 25 covers, 10½" × 14" navy and white cardboard holder with navy and white letters, 25 assorted drugstore matchbook covers **30.00**

Samples of medicine labels; prices vary according to size, intricacy, and contents.

Medicine bottle, 80-cc, 5¼" × 2" × 1¼"
clear, effervescent glass bottle, no name or
label, cork-stoppered empty bottle **7.00**

Collection #3
A Moderately Priced Collection

Browsers often become collectors as a result of receiving a present. A pharmacist's wife might purchase a Massey's drugstore bottle because her husband's grandmother once lived in Shirley, Indiana. He remembers tangy lemon phosphates served at Massey's Soda Fountain. On the pharmacist's next day off, both he and his wife return to the antique store from which they purchased the bottle. Their interest has been piqued and these two new collectors will begin to accumulate as many pieces as their space and budget will allow.

Pharmacy measure and stirrers, no name of company or location, liquid-medicine measure, 4-fl oz, 6¼ × 1½" round clear glass tapered to 3" measure, black measure lines and numbers, two 6¼" glass measures **15.00**

Pharmacy funnel, no name of company or location, for pouring liquid medicine from one container to another, 1-qt, 8½" × 6½" round clear glass funnel, "made in USA" etched near top rim **43.00**

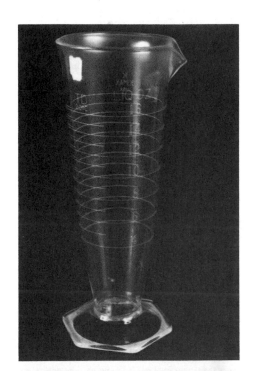

Pharmacy measure, Kimax, USA, no location, liquid-medicine measure, 16-fl oz, 9⅜" × 3½" round clear glass tapered to 1½" measure, white measure lines and numbers **10.00**

Advertising pharmacy bottle, R. A. Massey, registered pharmacist, Shirley, IN, "Massey's Drugstore prescription specialists," storage of liquid medicine, 16-fl oz, 9" × 2⅞" × 2" clear glass bottle, white label painted on front with white letters, empty bottle **12.00**

Advertising pharmacy bottle, Baltzly's, Massillon, OH, "economy prescription service," storage of liquid medicine, 6-fl oz, 6¼" × 2¼" × 1¼" clear glass bottle, white painted-on label with white letters, empty bottle **12.00**

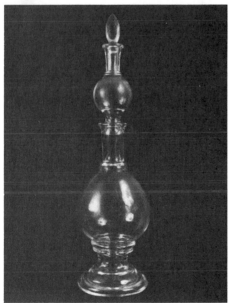

Showglobe, no name or location, holds colored water or pills for display, two parts, bottom section about 1 cup, top part section about 1 oz, clear glass, 13" tall, top globe 1½", bottom globe 3", glass stopper, no label or letters **55.00**

Collection #4
An Expensive Collection

An individual's interest would of course be the only constraint for anyone who could afford to amass a pharmaceutical collection in this price range.

Large iridescent showglobe, no name or location, holds colored water or pills for display, 5½" × 17½" clear glass showglobe, no label or letters, ground-glass swirl stopper **400.00**

Wooden mortar and pestle, used to grind or pound medicines, inner bowl is 5" × 4", overall height is 8" with 5" base, pestle is 8½" × 1½" **110.00**

Brass mortar and pestle, no name or location, for grinding medicine, 1-cup, 3¾" × 4½" round brass mortar, no label or letters, brass 6⅜" pestle, no label or letters **55.00**

Ceramic mortar and pestle, Blair, USA, "fashioned by Blair," for grinding medicine, 1-cup, 4" × 4¼" round white and gold ceramic mortar, gold trim and letters, 6½" ceramic gold-trimmed pestle **45.00**

Collectors' Resources

The following is a selected list of resources pertaining to the history and collecting of drugstore items. *Maloney's Antiques and Collectibles Resource Directory, 1994–1995,* by David J. Maloney Jr. (Wallace-Homestead, 1993), was invaluable to compiling this list. Maloney's guide is also an excellent resource for collectors in the medical and pharmaceutical fields who want to contact others with like interests.

Clubs/Associations

Maryland Microscopical Society
Dr. Sam Koslov
8621 Polk St.
McLean, VA 22102
Phone: 301-953-5591
Focuses on instruments and devices; medical, surveying, photographic, microscopical, navigational, horological, astronomical, etc.

Medical Collectors Association
Newsletter: *Medical Collectors Association Newsletter*
Dr. M. Donald Blanton, MD.
1300 Morris Park Ave.
Bronx, NY 10461

Medical Museums

The Country Doctor Museum
P.O. Box 34
Bailey, NC 27807
Phone: 919-235-4165

Hugh Mercer Apothecary Shop
% A.P.V.A.
1200 Charles St.
Fredericksburg, VA 22401
Phone: 703-373-3362

McDowell House & Apothecary Shop
125 S. Second St.
Danville, KY 40422
Phone: 606-236-2804

National Museum of Health & Medicine
Adrianne Noe, Curator
Bldg. 54
Walter Reed Medical Center
Washington, DC 20306
Phone: 202-576-2438 or 202-576-0401
FAX: 202-576-2164

Dental Museums

Dr. John Harris Dental Museum
1370 Dublin Dr.
Columbus, OH 43215
Phone: 614-486-2700
Mailing address is as above, but located in Bainbridge, Ohio

Medical University of South Carolina, Macaulay Museum of Dental History
171 Ashley Ave.
Charleston, SC 29425
Phone: 803-792-2288

Museum of Dentistry
295 S. Flower St.
Orange, CA 92668
Phone: 714-634-8944
FAX: 714-978-2686

National Museum of Dentistry
666 W. Baltimore St.
Baltimore, MD 21201
Phone 410-328-8314
FAX: 410-328-3028

Newsletter

Scientific, Medical & Mechanical
  Antiques
Greybird Publishing
Richard Van Vleck
11824 Taneytown Pike
Taneytown, MD 21787
Phone: 301-447-2680

Index

"Poison" labels, 9
Powders
  antiseptic, 30–31
  bath, women's, 102
  douche, 98
  foot, 37–39
  laxatives, adult, 57–59
  stomach, 87–88
  talcum, 70
  tooth, 27–28
Pregnancy medications, 98–99
Price removal, 5–6
Prices, 4, 9. *See also* Sample collections
Prophylactic items, 8, 11, 74–76
Props, movie, 3–4

Razor blades, men's, 68–69
Razors, men's, 69–70
Rectal products, 76–77
Reducing aids, 77
Reference books, pharmacy, 73–74
Remedies. *See* specific types
Reproductions, 7
Resources for drugstore collectibles, 132–133
Rheumatism remedies, 77–78
Rouge, 104
Rubs, 78–86
Rust, 5

Sample collections
  contemporary, 122–124
  expensive, 130–131
  inexpensive, 124–126
  moderately priced, 127–129
Sample description of drugstore collectibles,
    11–12
Sanitary products, women's, 99–100
Shampoo, women's, 106–107
Shaving cream, men's brushless, 67–68
Shaving products, men's, 67–70
Skin products
  infant and children, 48
  women's, 107–108
Stomach products, 86–91
  liquids, 87
  powders, 87–88
  tablets, 88–91
  use of, 86–87
Suntan products, 91–92
Suppositories
  hemorrhoidal, 76–77
  women's, 100, 102

Surgical appliances, 41–44
Syrups, cough and cold, 20–23

Tablets
  laxatives, adult, 59–64
  stomach, 88–91
Talcum, men's, 70
Teething products, 52
Throat medicines, 93–94
Throat products, 92–94
Tins, 9, 10
Toiletries. *See* Men's toiletries; Women's
    toiletries
Tonics, 94–96
Tooth pain relievers and accessories, 26
Toothpaste, 26
Tooth powders, 27–28
Topicals, antiseptic, 30–31
Trends in drugstore collectibles, 8–11

Urinary products, 54–55

Vaginal products, 99
Vermin remedies, 97–98
Videos of drugstore collectibles, 6
Vintage pharmaceuticals. *See* Drugstore
    collectibles; specific types
Vitamins
  adult, 94–96
  infant and children, 48–49

"Warehouse finds," 6
Weight loss aids, 77
Women's health and hygiene products
  demand for, 8–9
  douche powders, 98
  estrogenic hormones, 98–99
  labor medications, 98–99
  pregnancy medications, 98–99
  sanitary products, 99–100
  suppositories, 100, 102
  vaginal products, 99
Women's toiletries
  bath powders, 102
  cologne, 102
  cosmetics, 103–104
  creams, 107–108
  deodorant, 103
  hair products, 104–107
  lotions, 107–108
  skin products, 107–108
Wooden boxes, dovetail-jointed, 11